CALEB SUKO

Is God Calling Me to Missions?

10 Questions

to Help

Determine

Your Calling

Dovare Publishing

Is God Calling Me to Missions? 10 Questions to Help Determine Your Calling
Copyright © 2017 by Caleb Suko
Published by Dovare Publishing

Cover and interior design: Sergium
www.behance.net/sergiumstyle

Editor: Katie Alexson
www.katieaxelson.com

Print edition ISBN: 978-0-9994157-0-2

Thank you Duane Early for letting me see first hand the work of a faithful missionary!

Contents

Introduction

❝Is God calling me into missions?"

Young people often ask me how they can know if God is calling them into missions. It's a great question for anyone to ask themselves. Your understanding of this question and your answer to this question can dramatically affect the direction of your life.

There are few things sadder than to see a man or woman who heard God's call to missions early on in life, then either because they ignored that call, they fell into sin, or they found a spouse who didn't share their call they never went through with it. I pray that you will react and act quickly on God's call in your life. He may not be calling you to missions in a far off land but he is certainly calling you to some great and lasting work in his name!

Let's explore ten questions to help you understand the call and better determine how God is working in your life. This book is a tool to help you clarify the call on your life personally. Also I pray that in reading this material you will find a greater understanding of the call and you will develop a deeper passion to live out the call in your life. While I write this mainly with the call to missions in mind, certainly there are many aspects to the call that are general for all believers. For instance, we are all called to preach the gospel and make disciples (Matthew 28:16-20). However, we are not all called to cross borders and bring the gospel to foreign people. Whether or not God has called you into missions specifically I hope you'll find this book useful in understanding the call to preach the Good News of Jesus Christ.

While there are many instances in Scripture when God calls someone to go out as His representative and preach his truth, let's focus on the call of Isaiah the prophet. Isaiah's calling gives us unique insight to the heart of God and the task we are called to as missionaries. That being said, I do understand that Isaiah was more of a "home missionary." He was called to his own people, to his own culture. Isaiah didn't have to struggle with learning a new language or culture, but his task was at it's core the same as every missionary whom God calls.

It's also helpful to look at someone else's life on a practical level to see how these stories play out in a modern-day context. While I recognize our story is not as significant or shocking as Isaiah's, I share my family's story of being called into missions. Christina and I did not receive a direct revelation like Isaiah did, but God did call us to Ukraine. I hope that by reading it you will also find some common factors and be able to more clearly see God's calling in your life.

Importance of calling

Often young people make one of three mistakes when it comes to calling. The first mistake I call "follow the herd." They simply follow the masses. Their approach to the future isn't especially thought out but in general it goes like this:

1. Go to college and get a degree
2. Find a good job
3. Get married and have a family
4. Try to pay the bills for the rest of my life

While few would admit to "following the herd" the sad reality shows us that on a practical level many follow this pattern with no special purpose other than to get by, hopefully avoid trouble, and stay out of deep debt. Since you're reading this book I assume you have much higher aspirations.

There is a second mistake that others often make when it comes to calling; I call this mistake "stuck on the fence." These are the people who think God may be calling them but aren't quite sure. Since they can't yet determine God's clear direction they wait and do nothing. Not doing anything is one sure way to avoid ever seeing God's leading in your life. It's impossible to steer a boat that's dead in the water! Even Jonah could see God's hand pushing him toward Nineveh when he ran in the opposite direction.

We cannot ignore our calling or sit on the fence waiting for God to send us a calling engraved on stone tablets. In order to determine calling we need to carefully examine God's leading in our lives while actively pursuing ministry.

The third mistake when it comes to calling is the "lone ranger." The lone rangers are those who are so convinced they are called to a specific ministry in a specific place that they lack the patience and wisdom to listen to others around them who may be saying otherwise. Just as it would be a grave mistake to ignore God's calling in your life to missions, so also, it can be dangerous to pursue a ministry and calling that God has not given you.

Just as calling is important to the young as they set out to pursue God's lead in their life, so also calling is vital for those with years of experience. If you can investigate your calling now it will serve you well in the future. To be sure of your calling now means a much greater chance of long term service and faithfulness over decades rather than just a few years or months.

Many missionaries leave the field within the first 4-5 years. Often this is at least partly due to problems with their calling. Either they weren't called and decided to go anyway, or they were called but failed to see their calling clearly and when things got difficult on the mission field they grew discouraged and returned home.

When you have confidence in your calling it changes the way you view troubles and trials in ministry. Those who have forgotten how God called them will often see those trials as evidence that maybe God hasn't called them after all. On the other hand those who clearly saw God's calling will see the troubles as mere bumps in the road in their pursuit of that call.

On at least two occasions Paul reminded Timothy of the gifts God had given him and the laying on of hands from the elders as evidence of his calling to be a pastor and faithfully preach the gospel (1 Timothy 4:14, 2 Timothy 1:6). Paul knew this was a reminder Timothy needed on the tough days. Often it is this little reminder that will help us to push forward when ministry pushes us back and Satan tries to discourages us.

As a young man I didn't think that much about calling. I certainly didn't value calling as I do now, and I rarely took time to stop and exam-

7

ine God's working in my life in order to better follow His leading and hear His calling. The older I get and the more experience I receive in ministry, the more I value calling and see the significance of knowing your calling and following your calling over the long-term. I owe thanks to many people in my life especially my parents and members of my home church for helping me to see how God was calling me even as a teenager and then giving me the encouragement to pursue that calling. As I look back it's clear to me now how God was leading me but back then I was just taking a step at a time and hoping that I was going in the right direction.

Later on we will look in detail at Isaiah's call to missions which played a vital role in Isaiah's life and set the foundation for many decades of faithful ministry during difficult times. Isaiah's ministry was not "big and successful," yet he was faithful and never gave up. It is more likely God will call you to a ministry like Isaiah than to a "successful" ministry as man sees it. If we preach the gospel faithfully and accurately not many of us will see thousands or hundreds coming to Christ, not many of us will hear positive words of encouragement from the world around us. Most of us will be faced with great cause for discouragement; we will hear the disgust and anger of many; we will be asked to stop preaching; and we will be told that our message is insignificant, untrue, and lacks power. This is the reality of preaching the Gospel to a dying world.

Isaiah faced this reality head-on and remained faithful; he preached for 50-60 years with little success as man would define it! And yet, he continued to preach because he was confident in his God and secure in his calling! When we remember the God who called us and the calling he gave us, it changes everything; it gives us strength, endurance, and produces faithful missionaries in the face of adversity!

Our Story

Worlds Apart

I didn't really have a choice about going to church as a kid; my dad was the pastor so it was just something our family did. I'm thankful that God put me in a family where I often found myself surrounded by people who love Jesus. Certainly those men and women impacted my life positively in ways I still do not completely recognize.

My journey as a disciple of Jesus began shortly after my grandfather was diagnosed with cancer and given a short time to live. As a result I began asking my parents about what happens after death. They carefully and simply explained to me how I am a sinner and how Jesus died on the cross and rose again so that I could receive forgiveness. Although I had heard much about Jesus and the Bible I had never put faith in Jesus as God and Savior. At that time I realized the significance of Jesus sacrifice for me and I believed. It was the simple faith of a child that would grow in depth with time.

As a teenager I began to take on a few responsibilities in church. One of the first I remember was leading songs. I wasn't particularly gifted as a musician but I was willing. On Saturday evenings we would pick out the slides (literal slides that had to be organized and inserted into the projector). Then on Sunday mornings I would swing my arms to the beat and lead the worship.

One evening when I was 16 years old a missionary couple who served in Togo, West Africa came to speak in our church. Something about what they shared sparked a flame in my heart. After the service I asked them if there were any opportunities for missions that summer in Togo.

"I won't be there this summer," he told me, "But if you're interested I can find out if there are any other opportunities." I agreed; he would get back to me later with an opportunity that I could have never dreamed up.

Over 5,000 miles away a young girl went to one of the first Christian camps in the recently broken up former Soviet Union. After a week of hearing God's Word and listening to missionary stories they asked the young men and women who would like to give their lives in missionary service.

That young girl responded in faith to the call with no idea how God could use a simple girl from central Ukraine as a missionary. Fast forward about 5 years while Christina was busy serving in her church and working for a Christian publisher. She had almost forgotten about that night so many years ago when she responded to the call to missions. With little Biblical training and financial means it seemed very improbable now that she could serve as a missionary.

Then one day a missionary showed up looking for perspective young people to send to Bible college! He found Christina and within several months Christina found herself on a plane to Northern California.

An unexpected opportunity

Back in the States, I finally got news from my missionary friend. He called and told me there would be a missions conference at a nearby church soon and it would be good if I went to the closing service and talked with the main speaker. I went and honestly I can't remember what the sermon was about but I do remember talking to the preacher, his name was Wendell Kempton, who was then president of ABWE (Association of Baptist for World Evangelism).

I greeted him after the service and told him of my desire to serve for a month in the summer. "Caleb," he told me, "there's a great opportunity this summer in Ukraine!" It took me a second to figure out what country he was talking about as this was the early 90s and few people understood that Ukraine was a separate country from Russian and the Soviet Union.

His suggestion to go to Ukraine was not what I expected and not what I was looking for. My concept of missions included jungles and monkeys not apartment buildings and concrete.

"I'll pray about it," I told him, not completely enthrall with the news.

That night I went home and told my parents about the opportunity to serve for a month in Ukraine. When my dad heard about it quickly responded, "I'll come with you!" I wasn't sure what to do with that, I hadn't decided to go myself and my dad had already volunteered to come with me. Even though it wasn't what I was looking for I decided it was worth a try.

In less than less than a year I visited Ukraine twice. On our first trip we helped get things set up for the construction of a Bible training center. About 9 months later we made a second trip towards the end of the construction process. These trips were exciting and God taught me much through them about himself and about his church, yet I still did not believe God was calling me to Ukraine as a missionary.

Eventually I did find myself in the jungle, not in Africa but in South America. After highschool I traveled to Brazil where I lived with several different missionary families along the Amazon river. Once again God used this experience to give me a more in depth look at what it means to be a missionary.

No time for distractions

After 6 months in the jungles of Brazil I decided it was time for me to get some Biblical training. I chose a small Bible college in Northern California called Shasta Bible College. My older brother was also attending Shasta Bible College, and so my parents decided to go with me to help me get settled at the beginning of the school year.

At that time I remember talking with God, I asked him for 3 things. First, I asked him to help me not to get distracted from my studies by girls. Second, I told God that I would like to serve Him as a missionary part time. I thought I could earn money farming in the summers and then go on missions trips for the winter months. The third thing I told God was that I could serve Him in the ministry as long as I didn't have to preach. I was a quiet kid and couldn't comprehend how someone could speak for over 40 minutes on one verse of Scripture!

Just before the beginning of the academic year, while my parents were still visiting, the school held a picnic for all students, staff, and parents. Our school wasn't very big, around 80 students that year, which meant that it wasn't hard to get to know everyone in the school. Still it was the first event of the school year so I knew few of the other students.

After we came came home that evening we all went over to my brother's apartment and we were relaxing a little when my dad said, "Hey Caleb, I met this girl from Ukraine at the picnic, and I think you should marry her!" I laughed a little at the suggestion, after all I had already prayed that God wouldn't allow me to get distracted from my studies by girls.

Thankfully conversation quickly moved onto another topic and no one, including me, thought much more about my dad's comment. Just a few days later, however, I had chance to meet that girl from Ukraine and I immediately recognized the wisdom of my father's suggestion! By early November I picked up the phone and dialed my parents. "You know that girl from Ukraine?" I asked, "Well, I think I'm ready to be an obedient son!"

My parents were all for it, how could they not have been when it was my dad's idea in the first place? More importantly Christina and her parents were for it! As soon as the school year was over we jumped on a plane for Ukraine so I could get to know her parents better. A month later we were back in the Washington state where we wasted no time on getting married.

Our options are open

Even before we started dating and preparing for marriage we talked about our future. Christina shared with me her desire to serve the Lord as a missionary. I also told her about my experiences in Ukraine and South America. We realized that we both sensed God was leading us into missions; however, at that time neither of us knew exactly where we would serve or what we might do. I was thinking of possibly going back to the jungles of Brazil while Christina had Fiji on her mind because of a connection with a missionary there.

Shortly after we were married people would often say to us, "So you're going to Ukraine as missionaries?" At first we would awkwardly reply that we weren't quite sure but thought that possibly we would go to some other country. Nevertheless we kept our options open knowing that we still had time and that God would eventually make it clear to us.

I was starting to think that maybe God wanted me to serve on the mission field more than just a few months out of the year. Also as part of our Bible college studies I was required to take a preaching class. Something strange happened in that class, even though I had never really preached before and couldn't imagine speaking for more than 5-10 minutes at a time, some how I started to preach.

Time for training

After my first sermon I thought, "Well that must have just be a fluke because I don't know how I just did that!" Then it happened again and again. At the end of the year my fellow students nominated me for "Preacher boy of the year." Not that there was a big competition, we only had half a dozen guys in the class, however, the response of those who listened to my sermons helped me understand that maybe preaching was an area that God wanted to develop and use in my life.

When I entered Bible college I originally thought that one year of study should give me a sufficient foundation in the Bible. I was eager to get out there and serve and didn't want to be slowed down by years of schooling. However, as our first year of Bible college came to a close I realized that I still lacked much of what I needed to be effective in the ministry.

The more I studied the more I realized I didn't know, so after Bible college I decided to continue on to seminary. God showed me that these years of study and preparation were in no way wasted time. It was time that I need to grow in my knowledge of the Word and in my faith. It was also time when we could already engage in ministry.

While I was at Bible college I began doing pulpit fill for various small churches in the surrounding mountains of Northern California. This helped me learn the discipline of study and increased my skill in communicating God's Word. After college we moved up to Washington State where I attended Northwest Baptist Seminary in Tacoma, which was near my father's church.

This also proved to be a vital time of training. Since my father's church was close to the seminary he developed an internship program for seminarians. I spent 5 years ministering alongside my dad. Every few months he would rotate the responsibilities of each intern so that we could try out different ministries. He even had us interns sit in on the board meetings. I consider that time of practical training every bit as valuable as the theological and theoretical training that I received parallel to it. Between Bible college and seminary I spent a total of 9 years in school, and I consider none of that time wasted.

Visiting the in-laws

Of course I didn't forget about my in-laws in Ukraine after I got married! Despite all those years of school we still made time to visit Christina's family. We would save up our money and every year or two make a trip to Ukraine. At first it was mainly a family visit. Then we began to realize it was a long way to travel just to visit family, so maybe we should make ourselves useful in Ukraine just like we were in Washington.

Each time we visited we got involved in ministry, usually some kind of children's camps and preaching in various churches. We didn't realize at the time how God was going to use these experiences in our lives, not only as ministry training but also as a way to direct our hearts towards his calling in our lives.

Somewhere deep in our hearts we began to realize that maybe God wanted us to serve Him in Ukraine. I began to think this shortly after we moved from California to Washington for seminary studies. At first I didn't say anything to Christina knowing that she was thinking about becoming a missionary in Fiji. A few months went by and I finally decided to say something to her.

"It seems like maybe God is leading us to Ukraine," I said to her.

"Really?" she said, "That's what I've been thinking recently too."

When I heard that God was working in Christina's heart in the same way that he was working in my heart it both relieved a few worries and confirmed God's leading in our lives. Now we were starting to say the same thing that others had said to us a few years before, "So we're going to Ukraine as missionaries!"

Amazingly it took us a good 4 or 5 years to see what others recognized right away; God was calling us to come serve Him in Ukraine.

10 questions to determine your calling

Let's look at Isaiah 6, Isaiah's calling. As we break it down, take some time to prayerfully answer each question, write down your thoughts, and share your ideas with a trusted godly man or woman in your life. Doing this will certainly help you determine if, like Isaiah, God is calling you into missions.

Let's now look at our first question.

1. Are you in the right place?

God often calls into missions those who have placed themselves in the middle of God's will and who are passionately pursuing God's presence.

Look at where we find Isaiah when God called him.

In the year that King Uzziah died I saw the Lord sitting upon a throne, high and lifted up; and the train of his robe filled the temple. Isa 6:1

Isaiah was in the temple. The temple was the center for worship, it was also the place where God showed his mercy to man, and it was a reminder of God's saving power.

We don't know if Isaiah was literally in the temple. It could be that he just saw a vision of the temple; however, he gives us no reason to believe that he was not literally in the temple. Even if he wasn't in the temple, we can tell that Isaiah was very familiar with the temple and its furnishings. It was likely a place that he frequented in order to make his sacrifices and to worship his God.

What we find is that Isaiah put himself into a good position for God to call him. He put himself in place where God's presence uniquely dwelled, a place where worship, sacrifice, and prayer took place. He pursued God actively even when it wasn't popular in Judah.

What would that look like today? I think if Isaiah lived today he would have been active in his church, a present member who participated in ministry and engaged in the fellowship. The fact that Isaiah was in the temple tells us that he took his personal relationship with God seriously. He was familiar with God's Word and aware of the vital need of prayer.

We can look at this in two ways in our own lives. First, how are you placing yourself in God's presence personally? That is, are you taking your relationship with God seriously? Are you pursuing the Almighty through in-depth study of His Word and personal prayer? These elements of your spiritual life are vital now in order to build a strong foundation for future ministry.

In a personal letter Spurgeon gave this invaluable advice to a new missionary, which is just as valid for prospective missionaries:

> *"The Lord will be with you. Take special care to be much with HIM. Without the means of grace in the lone land as you will probably ere long, 'give attention to reading' the one and only book, and be often carried away to heaven on the wings of prayer and meditation."[1]*

I find that God often leads those best who are with Him most! A calling to missions will only be solidified and strengthened through regular personal Bible Study and prayer. Those who ignore this foundational aspect of the Christian life may feel a call but they will be less likely to listen and even if they do respond, they will find that the passion won't last.

The second aspect to be being in the right place, is finding yourself in the place of ministry even now. If you want to be successful on the mission field first learn to successfully minister on the home field. Look at how you can serve God in your local church and in your immediate context!

Every time I meet a young man or woman who tells me, "I want to serve the Lord in missions," I ask them, "How are your serving now? What kind of involvement do you have in your current church?" Sadly the answer is often underwhelming.

> "My church is small; there are no opportunities for ministry."
> "I'm not a member of the church where I go yet."
> "I would but I'm just very busy with other things."
> "Our church doesn't really do missions, so there's nothing for me to do."
> "They asked me to be involved in _____ but that's not my gift."

You can be sure that the difficulty of the task and the barriers you'll

---

1 C.H. Spurgeon, *The Letters of Charles Haddon Spurgeon*, ed. Iain H. Murray (Edinburgh: Banner of Truth Trust, 1992)

face in a foreign country and culture will be many times greater than those at home.

Have you ever met a professional football player who didn't start playing football until he was signed to a professional team? Of course not! Most of them spend years in training in amateur leagues refining their skills before they become professional. This principle is the same in missions, God often refines our character and strengthens our faith as we serve him in seemingly "insignificant" ministries.

This was an important part of my own calling. Even before I went on my first mission trip I began to serve in whatever capacity I could in our church. I participated in small groups, served as a leader in Awana, led music on Sunday mornings, and helped with the upkeep of the church facility. It seemed at the time that these were all small things but each experience was leading me in the right direction and making it easier for me to see God's will in my life.

If you want to serve badly enough you will find a place to serve in your church. If you believe God has called you to missions you must start by serving right here and right now! You need to stop waiting for that one big opportunity and start making use of the many small opportunities that God has placed right before you.

Friend, let me ask you, are you in the right place? Have you found a place for ministry where you are now? Are you in a place where there is worship, are you personally pursuing God's presence?

Follow up:
1. How are you currently involved in ministry?
2. How can you see your current ministry involvement as preparation for future missions service?
3. What are you doing to regularly pursue the presence of God in your life?
4. Talk with your pastor about opportunities for ministry in your local church.

2. Do you understand the holiness of God?

Maybe this seems like a strange question. I get it. It's easy to write off, "Of course I understand God's holiness" or "How does God's holiness relate to my calling as a missionary?" God's holiness was important to Isaiah's calling and it is important to yours also.

Above him stood the seraphim. Each had six wings: with two he covered his face, and with two he covered his feet, and with two he flew. And one called to another and said: "Holy, holy, holy is the LORD of hosts; the whole earth is full of his glory!" And the foundations of the thresholds shook at the voice of him who called, and the house was filled with smoke. Isa 6:2-4

Starting from verse 1 Isaiah gives us a vivid description of God sitting on His throne in the temple. This entire scene is meant to showcase God's holiness. In the midst of all that is going on, rushing wind from the seraph's wings, the smoke billowing out from inside the temple, there is an earth shaking rumble. This is not an earthquake; it is the sound of the seraphim calling out in chorus together, "Holy, holy, holy!"

The purpose of the seraphim is to focus Isaiah's attention on God's holiness. These seraphim could have focused Isaiah's attention on any number of aspects of God's nature. They could have said, "Love, love, love" or "Grace, grace, grace" or "Justice, justice, justice" but they didn't.

I believe God had them say "holy" because holiness is one key aspect of God's character and nature that seems to sum up many other aspects.

The holiness of God has three main aspects.
1. It speaks of "otherness." God is other; He is not like us; He is not like any animal or any other created thing.
2. It speaks of moral purity.
3. It speaks of something that is honored or set apart for special purposes.

Our problem with holiness is that we often see it as a stringent list of rules. To us it looks like a stuffy, tight collar, joyless type of living. Our problem with how we view holiness is that we look for it in the lives of people instead of in God's character.

A.W. Tozer wonderfully describes God's holiness this way:

"God's holiness is not simply the best we know infinitely bettered. We know nothing like the divine holiness. It stands apart, unique, unapproachable, incomprehensible and unattainable. The natural man is blind to it. He may fear God's power and admire His wisdom, but His holiness he cannot even imagine... Holy is the way God is. To be holy He does not conform to a standard. He is that standard. He is absolutely holy with an infinite, incomprehensible fullness of purity that is incapable of being other than it is. Because He is holy, His attributes are holy; that is, whatever we think of as belonging to God must be thought of as holy. God is holy and He has made holiness the moral condition necessary to the health of His universe."2

God's holiness is beautifully frightening and completely unlike anything our eyes have ever seen before! Your understanding of God's holiness is vital in missions. Without a deep and life changing view of God's holiness missions because little more than a humanitarian relief project with no eternal results!

John Piper brought the aspect of worship to the attention of many years ago in his book Let the Nations be Glad.

"Missions exists because worship doesn't. Worship is ultimate, not missions, because God is ultimate, not man. When this age is over, and the countless millions of the redeemed fall on their faces before the throne of God, missions will be no more."3

---

2 A.W. Tozer, *Knowledge of the Holy* (Reformed Church Publications, 2013), 84.

3 John Piper, *Let the Nations Be Glad* (Grand Rapids: Baker, 1993/2003), 17.

Piper accurately points out that worship is ultimate; it is what God wants and deserves from His creation. We do missions in order to make more worshippers of a God worthy of worship.

Missions exists because worship doesn't and worship doesn't exist because man doesn't understand the holiness of God. Without a proper view of God's holiness worship can never exist. To increase worship we must increase the knowledge of a holy God.

The call to missions is a call from a holy God to proclaim His holiness and in doing so create worshippers from all nations. God specifically gave Isaiah an opportunity to see His holiness up close; He knew this understanding would be vital to Isaiah's calling and to his future task.

The one called to missions must view that call in relation to the holiness of God. If God is not holy, there is no need for missions. If you do not have a deep understanding of God's holiness, you will neither see nor feel the dire need for missions. In order to more clearly hear the call of missions you must fix your gaze upon a holy God. In order to respond to the call to missions you must be able to communicate God's holiness to the world around you. It is God's holiness that tells us "Go and tell of a holy God, who is ready to judge but able to save!"

Follow up:

1. How would you describe the holiness of God based upon what you know about God's character?
2. How does understanding God's holiness practically motivate you towards missions?
3. What are a few ways you can increase your understanding of God's holiness?
4. Read A.W. Tozer's Knowledge of the Holy.

3. Do you understand the wretched nature of sin?

A growing horror over your own sin and sin in the world around you must be carefully cultivated along with your understanding of God's call to missions. We must understand that as missionaries we go as forgiven sinners to sinners who have not yet experienced God's grace.

A young man or woman who has just found forgiveness in Jesus Christ is rightly overwhelmed by God's grace and mercy to such an unworthy and and despicable soul. Yet give that same young person a dozen years of church going and moral reform and all too often you'll find a somewhat older and more put together church member who can't really remember the last time he did something truly "sinful." He's comfortable with his religious traditions and lacks a significant desire for either greater holiness or further removal from sin's rotting effects in his own life.

It's possible that Isaiah was exactly this kind of man. He was a "good man" with respect to others, he visited the temple and did his sacrifices and prayed his prayers. Yet he failed at a deeper level to understand how truly horrific his own sin was in contrast to the absolute holiness of God!

Notice Isaiah's reaction to God's holiness:

And I said: "Woe is me! For I am lost; for I am a man of unclean lips, and I dwell in the midst of a people of unclean lips; for my eyes have seen the King, the LORD of hosts!" Isa 6:5

Isaiah's reaction flows directly from his immediate experience with the overwhelming terror of an absolutely holy God. Instantly Isaiah sees a problem within himself and in the culture around him. He literally says, "I'm undone." He could see no way to go on living in the presence of such holiness. He was an unholy man living in an unholy world who now faced a holy God.

Tozer describes Isaiah's reaction this way:

"The sudden realization of his personal depravity came like a stroke from heaven upon the trembling heart of Isaiah at the moment when he had his revolutionary vision of the holiness of God. His pain-filled cry, "Woe is me! for I am undone; because I am a man of unclean lips, and I dwell in the midst of a people of unclean lips: for mine eyes have seen the King, the Lord of hosts," expresses the feeling of every man who has discovered himself under his disguises and has been confronted with an inward sight of the holy whiteness that is God. Such an experience cannot but be emotionally violent. Until we have seen ourselves as God sees us, we are not likely to be much disturbed over conditions around us as long as they do not get so far out of hand as to threaten our comfortable way of life."4

God's holiness gave Isaiah the proper perspective that he needed on his own life. Isaiah says he is "a man of unclean lips." He didn't say this because he had just finished eating and hadn't wiped his mouth yet. He didn't simply mean that he had a bad habit of saying curse words on an occasion. Isaiah refers to his lips and his words as evidence of the wretched state of his own heart.

"The good person out of the good treasure of his heart produces good, and the evil person out of his evil treasure produces evil, for out of the abundance of the heart his mouth speaks." Luk 6:45

Not only did Isaiah see clearly the wretched nature of his own heart but the horrific problem of sin in the society where he lived. Until you understand the desperately wicked nature of your own heart and of the world you can neither hear nor understand the call to missions.

I find there are two common problems when viewing the world around us. The first problem I call "Billboard blindness." If you drive

---

4 A.W. Tozer, *Knowledge of the Holy* (Reformed Church Publications, 2013), 83.

down the same road every day eventually you will become blind to many features alongside that road. For instance if you regularly drive a road lined with large billboards you might be hardpressed to tell someone what was on those billboards when you get to your destination. You have become so used to seeing them that you fail to take notice any more.

The frequency with which sin invades our minds on a daily and even hourly basis doesn't make us more sensitive to sin but rather tends to blind us to the true horror of sin. The unrelenting nature of sin numbs our minds to its presence and we fail to notice the process of corruption in the culture around us.

Part of the call to missions is becoming increasingly aware of the problem of sin in the world around us. Isaiah saw sin clearer than he had ever seen it before. He now saw sin in contrast to God's holiness. Billboard blindness can be overcome when we stop, get out of our car and shine the light of God's Word upon those billboards.

Since you are unlikely to have a vision of a holy God like Isaiah had, you must find another way to cultivate your awareness of surrounding sin. God's Word is the primary source you and I can go to in order to find God's holiness. It is in his Word that we find descriptions of God's holiness like we have here in Isaiah 6. We also come to know of God's power, judgement, and wisdom, which are all aspects of His holiness. Careful study of God's Word accompanied by personal prayer, and sincere worship all help us gain a proper perspective of our fallen world.

The second problem is how we often view sin in the world around us. It's not difficult to see that our world has problems. Just turn on the news on any given evening and you'll find many stories of war, crime, and other tragic events. You probably don't have to travel too far from your home to find neighborhoods where people live in poverty, illegal drug use is prevalent, and houses are in a state of disrepair.

Often these visible problems multiply on the mission field. It's easy to look at these obvious needs and determine that you will focus your efforts on fixing them. While certainly as disciples of Christ we must show our Savior's love by helping those in need, there is also a danger here that we must be careful to avoid.

Unfortunately today too many people see missions as mainly about "fixing" things. People go on missions to build houses for the poor, to provide healthcare to the sick, or to dig wells for the thirsty. These are all good things, even great things; they are helpful, and they can certainly be part of what a missionary does but they are not the primary call or motivation for going.

We must carefully separate the call of missions from the humanitarian call to "fix" what is broken in our society. The call to missions must primarily deal with an evil and broken heart. The called missionary is one who first has come to terms with his own evil heart. The heart doesn't need a better house, warmer clothes, or cleaner water; it needs Jesus!

We are called to bring God's offer of healing and forgiveness to sinful people. One way that we do this is by giving them real examples of love and compassion such as caring for their physical needs. However, we must never forget that the needs of the world around us go far deeper than financial poverty and far broader than physical diseases. The called missionary sees the depravity of the human heart in contrast to the holiness of the Almighty God.

Follow up:
1. How would you describe man's deepest and greatest problem?
2. How does helping people with visible needs fit into the mission call?
3. What are some ways you can develop a sensitivity to sin in your own heart?
4. Read and and meditate on David's psalms of repentance (Psalms 51, 52, 53)

4. Has God prepared you?

Thankfully God did not leave Isaiah to wallow in the soil of his own sin and he does not leave us there either! In the next two verses we see how God prepared Isaiah for his missionary service.

Then one of the seraphim flew to me, having in his hand a burning coal that he had taken with tongs from the altar. And he touched my mouth and said: "Behold, this has touched your lips; your guilt is taken away, and your sin atoned for." Isa 6:6-7

What happens in these two verses paints a vivid picture of God's ability to remove our guilt. In line with Isaiah's statement, "I'm a man of unclean lips" the Seraph touches a coal to the lips of Isaiah signifying God's forgiveness and purification. After this experience I'm sure Isaiah had no doubt about where he stood. He stood firmly before God a forgiven man!

The call to missions comes only to those who have been properly prepared by God himself. We don't know exactly what preparation Isaiah had before this, likely Isaiah already believed in the One true God. However, it seems that Isaiah lacked a true and profound understanding of his own salvation. After seeing God in all his holiness it was necessary to remind Isaiah of God's provision of forgiveness and salvation to those who humbly seek Him and believe in Him.

God calls no one to missions without this important preparation. Maybe it goes without saying, but this one is too important to simply assume; you must experience God's forgiveness personally if you want God to send you to tell others about that forgiveness! If you have doubts in your heart about your personal salvation then you need to stop now and take care of that disbelief before entering into missionary service.

Sadly, there are many who go as "missionaries" who have not yet experienced God's grace in their own lives. The Wesley brothers are two historic examples. In 1735 both Charles and John Wesley sailed from England to America on a mission trip. While in America they tried desperately to preach the Gospel to Native Americans. However, they found little success and left America discouraged and dismayed by their lack of success.

On the voyage home John wrote in his journal:

"I went to America, to convert the Indians; but oh! who shall convert me? who, what is he that will deliver me from this evil heart of mischief? I have a fair summer religion. I can talk well; nay, and believe myself, while no danger is near; but let death look me in the face, and my spirit is troubled. Nor can I say, 'To die is gain!'"[5]

"It is now two years and almost four months since I left my native country in order to teach the Georgian Indians the nature of Christianity. But what have I learned myself in the meantime? Why (what I the least of all suspected), that I who went to America to convert others was never myself converted to God. 'I am not mad,' though I thus speak; but 'I speak the words of truth and soberness'; if haply some of those who still dream may awake and see that as I am, so are they."[6]

It was plainly obvious even to John himself that he did not posses a genuine faith in Jesus Christ. He was struggling to convert the Georgian Indians to a way of life, to a Christian culture rather than exhorting them to cast all their faith upon a risen Savior. If you lack confidence in your Savior or if you waver in your conviction of God's personal saving power towards you then you will surely go home from the mission field discouraged and dismayed.

The called missionary must go in absolute assurance of his position before God. He must be convinced from head to toe that God has forgiv-

---

5 John Wesley's journal, January 24th 1738

6 John Wesley's journal, January 29th 1738

en him of his sins, saved him from coming punishment, and given him a promised inheritance in heaven. He must boldly walk in the knowledge of salvation by faith alone in Christ alone. A rock solid confidence in the Rock of our salvation provides the necessary foundation for successful missionary service.

Shortly after the Wesley's came back to England they both began to talk with a Moravian missionary named Peter Bohler. It was Bohler who explained to them the concept of salvation by faith alone in Christ alone. In a large part as a result of Bohler's patient gospel teaching eventually both John and his brother Charles came to faith in Jesus Christ. John later wrote about his conversion:

"In the evening I went very unwillingly to a society in Aldersgate Street, where one was reading Luther's preface to the Epistle to the Romans. About a quarter before nine, while he was describing the change which God works in the heart through faith in Christ, I felt my heart strangely warmed. I felt I did trust in Christ, Christ alone for salvation; and an assurance was given to me that he had taken away my sins, even mine, and saved me from the law of sin and death." 7

The story of the Wesley brothers give reminds us that sometimes we can deceive ourselves, it shows us that the best intentions toward missionary service and pleasing God do not guarantee our own salvation. The call to missions must be preceded by genuine faith in the genuine Savior; Jesus Christ. I do not advise anyone to head out on a missionary journey whose faith is weak and who is not yet firm in the confidence of his or her own salvation.

Dear reader, has God prepared your heart? Have you come to God in humble repentance and genuine faith in Jesus Christ? The call to missions comes to those who have a prepared heart and it comes to those who learn to grow in their astonishment of the grace that has been given them.

---

7 John Wesley's journal, May 24th 1738

Follow up:

1. Are you trusting in Jesus alone for your forgiveness and salvation?
2. Consider making an in-depth study of the Gospel of John.
3. If you have doubts about where you stand before God, talking with your pastor.
4. Read J.D. Greear's book, Stop Asking Jesus into Your Heart.

5. Do you understand the nature of the call?

Often people ask, "God, are You calling me to missions?" But maybe this isn't exactly the right approach. What we find in Isaiah's case is quite the opposite, here it's not Isaiah asking the question but God!

And I heard the voice of the Lord saying, "Whom shall I send, and who will go for us?" Then I said, "Here I am! Send me." Isa 6:8

First, notice that the call to missions is from God. That fact alone should be enough to make us listen very closely! It is God doing the calling and He's asking for volunteers who are prepared to go in the name of the King of Kings! If you are ready then why wouldn't you go? A call from God is the highest call possible, it is the greatest honor that can be given to man!

Some might say they are called to be a fireman, a doctor, a teacher, or a builder. These are all good and noble professions that provide necessary services to our world. However, the call to missions supersedes them all. This in no way means that a missionary is a higher rank of Christian than a policeman or a chief. What it means is that if God has called you to missions it must always take priority in your life over all professions.

Take for instance Isaiah. While Isaiah may have been in employed in some worthy profession before his call we sense from his response that he was ready to drop it all and pursue God's call to missions. Sometimes the call to missions requires us to leave behind our profession and sometimes it doesn't. When Jesus called the disciples to follow Him they left behind everything!

And he said to them, "Follow me, and I will make you fishers of men." Immediately they left their nets and followed him. Mat 4:19-20

On the other hand the Apostle Paul was able to use his profession as a way to fund his missionary travels. It appears that Paul often worked making tents during the week so that he could preach the Gospel on Sabbaths.

And he found a Jew named Aquila, a native of Pontus, recently come from Italy with his wife Priscilla, because Claudius had commanded all the Jews to leave Rome. And he went to see them, and because he was of the same trade he stayed with them and worked, for they were tentmakers by trade. And he reasoned in the synagogue every Sabbath, and tried to persuade Jews and Greeks. Act 18:2-4

Paul even reminds the church in Thessalonica how he worked hard night and day so as not to be a financial burden on them. (I Thessalonians 2:9) One called to missions must be ready to leave his profession behind or if needed, engage in a new profession that will enable him to pursue missions. The call to missions is not a professional call but a divine call and thus it intersects and supersedes all other calls in the missionary's life.

Second, if we understand that the call to missions is truly from God then we must realize that to ignore the call is dangerous. Let's not forget our friend Jonah who ignored God's call and was suddenly swallowed by a fish! No matter how difficult the ministry, it is always better to listen and go than to ignore God's call. There are many reasons for missionaries to ignore their call.

Even if you are walking close to God spiritually, there may be an aspect of fear that comes along with the call to missions. God can call you to a dangerous place or even to a an unfamiliar place. Remember there are are few things Satan hates more than a heart willing and ready to preach the gospel in foreign lands! I have witnessed many occasions where the call to missions is followed by great hardship, sickness, family problems, legal problems, and more. With these kind of barriers in our way it can be tempting to give up and ignore the call God has given you. However, we must realize that it will always be much better for us in the end to ignore Satan's attacks and closely follow God than to give in to

Satan's attacks and ignore God!

Third, you should know that the call does not guarantee you "success." It's easy to look at a prophet like Isaiah and think that he was a success. However, I'm sure that nearly everyone who knew Isaiah would tell you that Isaiah was not a successful prophet. Year after year he preached and few listened and even fewer responded. Yet, no one can say that Isaiah wasn't called by God. Isaiah received a clear personal call from God Himself which he heard with his own ears while standing in God's presence. God may call you to a ministry like Isaiah's where few listen, it may not be successful in the the eyes of the world around you, but as long as you are faithful like Isaiah, then it will be successful in God's eyes!

Despite the fact that so few responded to Isaiah in his day we know that his faithful ministry produced amazing results. Isaiah left behind the one of the greatests books of prophecy. Because of his writings many people were able to correctly identify the Messiah after He came. His prophecies have strengthened the faith of millions of Christians and likely have also brought millions to a saving faith in Jesus Christ.

Fourth, do not forget that the call is spiritual. We are not called to build church buildings, hospitals, start new programs, or even to feed the poor. The call of the missionary is a spiritual call, it is a call to preach the Gospel, to turn men and women to Jesus, to make clear the truth of salvation, to exhort others to repent of their sins and believe in Christ. While we might use all the methods I mentioned, we must remember that we are not called to a method or specific ministry approach but rather to the simple and pure work of preaching the Gospel. This focus should be guarded above all else.

Follow up:
1. Why is the call to missions primary?
2. How could your current profession help or hinder you in the missionary endeavour?
3. How would you define "success" in missions?
4. For a good example of the primacy of the Gospel in ministry, read The Gospel Focus of Charles Haddon Spurgeon

6. Do you have a desire to go?

It wasn't the live coal that changed Isaiah but rather the forgiveness that he knew God had given him when that burning coal touched his lips. We can see the change in Isaiah by his two contrasting responses to God. His first response to God's holiness was negative, "I'm undone!" now when God asks for volunteers we see Isaiah jumping up and down like a school boy with his hand raised high in the air!

"Pick me, pick me, pick me!"

...Then I said, "Here I am! Send me." Isa 6:8

I'm convinced that righteous desires can only come from God. Satan isn't in the business of tempting people to give their lives to missions. Unfortunately there are times when we can confuse a true desire for missions with other desires that do not arise from proper Biblical motivation for missions. Some people desire adventure and the romance of traveling to new places, some may go to the mission field in an effort to meet the expectations of others, while still more may be trying to win God's grace and by becoming a missionary.

To go with misplaced desires is dangerous. It will most likely result in lost passion, discouragement, and return home sooner than expected. However, a Biblically informed desire will never point you in the wrong direction and will provide you with the strength needed when you find that "missions" is not a romantic travel adventure! The substance of your missions desire and passion must firmly connect with your understanding of God and the forgiveness he has given you through Jesus Christ.

Pastor John Piper explains the question of desire for missions this way:

"To be sure, as you discern God's call on your life, take into account your gifts, consider the need, consult your church. But in the end, the question is this: Is there an unrelenting, recurring, desire

to spend and be spent for the glory of Christ among unreached peoples of the world?" 8

While a desire to go is a good sign that God has called you, the absence of that desire does not automatically mean you are not called. Once again let's not forget Jonah! We know that God called him (Jonah 1:2) and Jonah's response was to get up and run the other way (Jonah 1:3)! Why didn't Jonah's desire line up with God's call to missions in his life? Most likely it was because Jonah's understanding of God's salvation plan was out of whack. Unlike, Isaiah, Jonah did not have a Biblical outlook on his own position before God and upon God's grace and mercy. It is only when we succeed in aligning our correct knowledge of a holy God with reality that God can begin the work of creating those righteous desires in us.

Isaiah's new-found desire to serve God flowed directly from his understanding of what God had done for him. Isaiah wasn't looking for an adventure, trying to earn God's favor, or seeking to meet the expectations of his friends or family. It was a pure holy desire to share with others the joy that God had given him. This should be the primary and ever growing factor that pushes your hand into the air and says,

"Pick me, pick me!"

What exactly does a righteous desire for missions look like? Let's look at a few characteristics to help you identify it.

A thankful heart

Gratitude should never be an empty word nor an idle feeling for the child of God. It was thankfulness that energized Isaiah to boldly say, "Here am I, send me!" The desire to serve in missions must connect with a heart overflowing with thanksgiving. We go not because we "must" or

---

8 John Piper, "May I Help You Discern Your Calling?", (http://www.desiringgod.org/articles/may-i-help-you-discern-your-calling, retrieved, May 16, 2016)

"should" or "have to" but because we "get to," because we want to more than anything else!

Like a child who received the toy he had been longing for at Christmas we must jump to our feet and embrace our Heavenly Father!

A readiness to serve God

Missions involves serving people yet it is primarily about serving and pleasing God. A desire for missions must include an eagerness to do all you can to please your loving and holy God. You are not earning His favor but rather returning His favor.

Notice what Isaiah didn't say.

He didn't say:
"Here am I, please don't send me."
"Here am I, I'll go if no one else does."
"Here am I, I suppose I could go for a few months."
"Here am I, I'll go if it's not too hard."
"Here's my friend Bob, why don't you send him?"

Isaiah's exact words were, "Here am I, send me!" In one short sentence Isaiah threw himself upon the altar of God's will, he held nothing back, he was ready to serve God whenever, wherever, for however long needed! He did not limit his involvement, he did not hold back parts of his life, he did not leave himself a "Plan B." He so fully committed himself to service of God that he didn't even pause after saying, "Here am I" to see what God's answer would be, instead he boldly made the suggestion, "Send me!"

A love for God's Word

God's Word is the core of all that a missionary does. Without a deep and abiding love for God's Word it is impossible to have a godly desire for missions. Isaiah indicates his value for God's Word in just about every corner of his book. Very early on in the book he writes:

Hear, O heavens, and give ear, O earth; for the LORD has spoken... Isa 1:2

This kind of statement tells us of the authority Isaiah invested in God's Word. "Jehovah has spoken" indicates divine revelation; it is something that should be listened to very carefully and then obeyed. Later in the book Isaiah will tell us other important facts about God's Word.

The grass withers, the flower fades, but the word of our God will stand forever. Isa 40:8

For as the rain and the snow come down from heaven and do not return there but water the earth, making it bring forth and sprout, giving seed to the sower and bread to the eater, so shall my word be that goes out from my mouth; it shall not return to me empty, but it shall accomplish that which I purpose, and shall succeed in the thing for which I sent it. Isa 55:10-11

A love for God's Word must accompany the desire to serve in missions!

A love for God's people

Isaiah's ministry was not an easy one, few people responded but God did promise him that there would be a remnant, a small percentage of people who would turn in faith to God, these are God's people.

And though a tenth remain in it, it will be burned again, like a terebinth or an oak, whose stump remains when it is felled." The holy seed is its stump. Isa 6:13

It was for this holy seed that Isaiah went out and preached. As a missionary you will preach the gospel to many and not all will respond, yet some will, they are the reason we go out, they are the reason we don't give up, they are worth the pain and the problems that you will face as a missionary!

The Apostle Paul also describes a similar desire in himself:

Therefore I endure everything for the sake of the elect, that they also may obtain the salvation that is in Christ Jesus with eternal glory. 2Ti 2:10

The reward for the missionaries work is growth of the church, if you don't love God's people, if you are not enthralled with the Church then your desire for missions is off.

A recognition of spiritual darkness

Recognizing the veil of darkness that covers the unbelieving heart is also a vital part of the missionaries desire to go. The missionary understands that without Christ man is in complete darkness. We don't simply go to fix social problems, we take the light of God into a dark hearts.

Later Isaiah describes the darkness that envelops the people to whom he is being called to preach. Notice that they are not only "in" darkness but the darkness is also "in them."

And when they shall say to you, Seek to the mediums and to wizards who peep and mutter; should not a people seek to their God, than for the living to the dead? To the Law and to the testimony! If they do not speak according to this Word, it is because no light is in them. And they shall pass through it, hard-pressed and hungry; and it shall be, they shall be hungry; They shall rave and curse their king and their God, and look upward. And they shall look to the land; and behold, trouble and darkness and gloom of anguish! And they are driven away into darkness. Isa 8:19-22[9]

---

9 Modern King James Version, (Sovereign Grace Publishers, January 1993).

God called Isaiah to preach to people who were in darkness and in whom darkness dwelled. After being exposed to the light of God's holiness Isaiah now had a basis to see this darkness as it was, hideous, dangerous, and far from God. His task to shed light on blackened hearts would not be easy. Many would shrink further into the darkness, some would try to put out the light that Isaiah carried. Yet Isaiah could also see that the end result of this darkness, it would bring destruction and anguish upon the people. Certainly Isaiah also remembered the darkness that previously dwelt in his own heart. This knowledge surely strengthened his desire to go with the light of God's Word, after all, only divine light could dissipate the spiritual darkness of the human heart.

In the gospels we see Jesus coming as the "true light" (John 1:4-5) and "the light of the World" (John 8:12, 12:46). Jesus also teaches us how we ought to be the light and gives us one compelling reason to bring God's light into a dark world.

In the same way, let your light shine before others, so that they may see your good works and give glory to your Father who is in heaven. Mat 5:16

The reason is simple, we want others to enjoy the treasure of God, we want them to join us in glorifying and worshiping the one true God forever. The only way for that to happen is to bring them the light of the gospel!

A disregard for personal power, position, or praise

On the negative side it's also helpful to look at what is not included in the desire for missions. Isaiah's response to God's call is simple and pure. He does not appear to be vying for position, trying to "move up the ladder," or anticipating some sort of authority or power.

Isaiah seemed to be well acquainted with the authorities of his day, he interacted with kings. It appears that Isaiah may have been been of royal blood, Jewish traditions holds that Isaiah's father was the brother of King Amaziah. If that's true then Isaiah would have known a lot about positions of power. Like any government modern or ancient, struggles for power are common. Isaiah quite likely had "connections" in the king's palace who, if he wanted them to, could "get things done."

Yet we sense no greed for power in Isaiah's voice as he volunteers for service of the Almighty God; we see no political ambitions or maneuvering for a better position in the monarchy. In fact, what we see is quite the opposite. Isaiah's message would not be a positive one for the rulers of his day to hear. His message would cause him problems personally; it would take from him any political power that he may have had.

Unfortunately our propensity towards power and popular positions can easily be passed off as a genuine passion for missions. In Western church culture missionaries are often elevated far above what is proper, because they have "sacrificed" everything for the mission. While we should respect those who choose to give their lives in service to God in another country, we must at the same time never allow the praise and admiration of man nor the opportunity for power and position to play a role in our desire for missions. Your desire for missions must chart a wide course around personal fame, power, and praise.

A secondary regard for the conditions of service

By secondary conditions of service I mean the following things and those like them:

How much will I get paid?
What kind of house will I live in?
What kind of health insurance will I have?
What kind of retirement package will they give me?
Etc...

Certainly all the things mentioned above have a level of importance and can greatly affect our ministries. However, we must also understand that they are secondary to our call. That is to say, these conditions do not have a direct relation to our call but only a secondary effect on the details of our service to God.

Notice that Isaiah doesn't have any criteria for serving God. He doesn't say, "I'll go if you can promise a decent salary, and a good retirement plan." Isaiah's desire to go and to serve his God is so powerful that he's not afraid to answer the call before knowing all the details.

A wise missionary will pay attention to the details of his service. He must take care of the proper paperwork if visas are necessary, he must make sure his family is provided for, that they have funds to properly feed and clothe themselves and continue in ministry. Yet these questions must always have a secondary nature in the heart of the called missionary.

J.C. Ryle puts it well:

"Zeal in Christianity is a burning desire to please God, to do His will, and to advance His glory in the world in every possible way. It is a desire, which is not natural to men or women. It is a desire which the Spirit puts in the heart of every believer when they are converted to Christ, however, a desire which some believers feel so much more strongly than others that they alone deserve to be called "zealous" men and women. This desire is so strong, when it really reigns in a person, that it impels them to make any sacrifice-to go through any trouble-to deny themselves anything to suffer, to work, to labor, to toil, to spend themselves and be spent, and even to die-if only they can please God and honor Christ." 10

We desire to go not because the pay is good and the living arrangements are comfortable but because deep within rests a desire to please our Savior! When knowing God and making Him known is your greatest pursuit you'll find serving Him, no matter the situation your greatest satisfaction. Our God is a Father who wants to give us righteous desires and then help us fulfill those desires for his glory!

Follow up:
1. How would you describe a Biblical desire for missions in your own words?
2. After reading this section do you believe God has given you personally a desire for missions? Why or why not?

---

10 J.C. Rylem "Christian Zeal" (http://www.biblebb.com/files/ryle/zeal.htm, retrieved May, 2017).

3. What other factors might give you either a false desire for missions or keep you from having a desire for missions all together?
4. Read Christian Zeal by J.C. Ryle.

7. Do you understand the task before you?

Although Isaiah doesn't demand details before commiting to the missions call go, God does not leave him without instruction on his task.

And he said, "Go, and say to this people: "'Keep on hearing, but do not understand; keep on seeing, but do not perceive.' Make the heart of this people dull, and their ears heavy, and blind their eyes; lest they see with their eyes, and hear with their ears, and understand with their hearts, and turn and be healed." Isa 6:9-10

God responds to Isaiah giving him some details about the task before him. Let's break that task down into its primary parts. Very simply we can see three aspects to the missions task: going, telling, and persevering.

"Going"

Before God instructs Isaiah on what he should say or how he should say it, he tells him "Go." While certainly missions is much more than simply traveling, we also must not overlook this vital aspect of the missions call.

Early on in Scripture we see examples of prophets "going" out from the Lord. One of the earliest examples is Abraham, who was not only a patriarch but also a prophet (Genesis 20:7), God told him to "go" from his own country and from his own culture to a place where God would show him (Genesis 12:1). As we see often in Scripture, the act of going is a significant expression of faith in the One who is sending.

In Abraham's case going out from his homeland was not only uncomfortable, it was dangerous. Abraham would need to move his entire family with all their flocks, herds, servants, and tents. Beyond the regular risk of traveling across open wilderness, being attacked by wild animals, or running out of basic supplies, there was the risk of other nations through whose land they must travel. Abraham already had some wealth and as his clan moved across the land the locals would view him as a risk to their safety.

When Abraham left his homeland he made a bold and shocking statement, it was a public declaration of his faith in Yahweh, who would protect him and provide for him as he went out, it was also a rejection of his family's pagan religion. The called missionary must make a similar step of faith. Unique to the missions call is the aspect of going, not all are required to go to far off lands but all missionaries are required to go somewhere!

Let's look at the first missionaries in Acts:

While they were worshiping the Lord and fasting, the Holy Spirit said, "Set apart for me Barnabas and Saul for the work to which I have called them." Then after fasting and praying they laid their hands on them and sent them off. So, being sent out by the Holy Spirit, they went down to Seleucia, and from there they sailed to Cyprus. Act 13:2-4

Notice in the above brief description how many times it refers to the "going" aspect of missions. It says the people "let them go," they were "sent out by the Holy Spirit," and they "went down." Why is going a vital aspect of the missions call? Certainly going is a strong statement of the missionary's faith in the One who is sending him, yet there is more to it than just that.

Going, is vital because the missionary is called to bring the gospel message to a people who are in darkness. Even with the advance of technology, with the ability to record video, publish blog posts, or produce podcasts, God still wants people to represent him personally. We can and should use all available technologies to communicate the gospel, but we must never be content with that alone!

God Himself communicated with us through written word, He used prophets as communicators of His message, yet when it came down to it, when the most important truths had to be communicated He did it personally, He sent His one and only Son as Word incarnate.

The true light, which gives light to everyone, was coming into the world. He was in the world, and the world was made through him, yet the world did not know him. He came to his own, and his own people did not receive him. Joh 1:9-11

Jesus came as the ultimate missionary; He went from the presence of the Father to the humble life of a servant (Philippians 2:5-8). We go as ambassadors of God (2 Corinthians 5:20) seeking the lost and the broken and personally communicating the message of hope to them.

In order to understand properly the missionary call you must not overlook the "going" of the missionary. It is impossible for a missionary not to go in some sense of the word. Some will travel to the other side of the globe, while others will find their "going" much nearer. Isaiah, for example, was told to go to the people of Judah. This meant that Isaiah would stay within the borders of his own country. However, he still needed to "go."

Telling

While "going" is usually the missionary's first task, it is not his primary task. Going is a necessary aspect of of telling. Paul shows us how going and telling work together to accomplish God's purposes.

...How then will they call on him in whom they have not believed? And how are they to believe in him of whom they have never heard? And how are they to hear without someone preaching? And how are they to preach unless they are sent? As it is written, "How beautiful are the feet of those who preach the good news!" Rom 10:13-15

True faith and heart change can only happen as a result of the "preaching" or "telling" of the Good News! Friend, do not let your heart forget the central assignment of every missionary, we are sent to deliver truth and hope to a dying world. We are at our core story tellers, news proclaimers, truth communicators. Above all the missionary must concern himself with the communication of God's revelation. Words of truth, salvation, and faith must flow fearlessly, flawlessly and frequently from the missionary's mouth.

The responsibility to communicate is the main reason why language learning is so crucial to missions. I found that successful missionaries are the ones who have never grown content with their ability to communicate in the heart language of those they serve but are continually seeking to improve. Not only do good language skills allow the missionary to survive in his new country but more importantly they allow him to communicate the gospel with greater accuracy.

Certainly we can and must communicate in ways that go beyond language. We use body language, facial expressions, and acts of kindness, yet we must always come back to the specific words and their arrangement in language as the main medium of communication in all cultures and countries. God made us a talking people, he designed us with a deep need and ability to communicate issues of the heart and soul through our words.

The goal of a missionary is to communicate the gospel message as accurately and understandably as possible in his given culture and language. In order to do this he must invest, thousands of hours into learning this new language and culture. The truth is that culture and language can not be separated. You can learn about another culture without learning their language, but you can not truly learn a culture with its thousands of nuanced shades of meaning and near endless connotations without learning the language.

The missionary task is one of telling good news, therefore he must be prepared to focus his time and energy on the learning the communicate accurately and understandably in his ministry context.

Isaiah's main task was to preach God's Word to the people, to warn them of coming judgment and call them to repentance. For the New Testament believer the basic task is the same. We are called to warn people of God's wrath against sin and exhort them to turn in repentance to Jesus Christ.

Persevering

God is upfront with Isaiah; He lets Isaiah know right away that there will be very few who respond to his preaching. Isaiah is instructed to tell the people:

...Keep on hearing, but do not understand; keep on seeing, but do not perceive. Isa 6:9

It's obvious that there will not be an immediate positive response to the message God has given Isaiah. In fact God tells Isaiah to literally:

Make the heart of this people dull, and their ears heavy, and blind their eyes... Isa 6:10

This not only informs us about the calloused and indifferent response of the people but also helps us understand Isaiah's task better. God called Isaiah to persevere in ministry, it wouldn't be enough for him to preach one day, one month, or even one year. Isaiah must persist in his task; he must make their hearts fat with his preaching and their ears heavy.

More often than not the mission task is one of years and decades and not one of days and months. How many thousands of missionaries have gone home discouraged and dispirited after only a few months or a few years of service? Could it be that they did not understand the mission's task and that misunderstanding resulted in their dismay, which eventually sent them home? I'm afraid that this is sometimes the case.

Friend, as you think about missions do not be misled with ideas of great success and enthusiastic responses to the gospel message. Yes, there are times when the Spirit moves and great revivals takes place, however, all revivals are preceded by years of faithful and difficult mission service with little visible fruit. We ought to pray with tears and heartfelt passion for revival to happen in our days, yet we must not be so presumptuous to assume that we are guaranteed this type of response if our faith is great enough, our prayers are strong enough, and our ministry is good enough.

It would be unwise to say that any of us are greater preachers than

Isaiah and yet, he saw no revival in his day. Nevertheless he was persistent in his work and faithful in his task, this is what God requires of a missionary.

Our job is to preach faithfully and we should evaluate our ministries by faithfulness not by the number of people who responded positively, the quantity of tracks we've handed out, or the size of the church building we built. Yes, we want to see many respond in faith and it is a great blessing from God when that happens, nevertheless our focus should be squarely on the task of clearly and faithfully communicating God's truth to lost people.

Follow up:
1. Why is going important to missions?
2. How would you describe the central task of missions?
3. Why do you think God warned Isaiah about the people's response? How might that warning apply to your ministry?
4. Read Liberating Ministry from the Success Syndrome R. Kent Hughes and Barbara Hughes

8. Have you prayed about it?

Looking at Isaiah 6 you might be tempted to say that Isaiah didn't need to pray about his call. However, if we correctly understand what prayer is then we realize that Isaiah's vision happens in the context of prayer. The vision took place in the temple, which Isaiah refers to as a "house of prayer."

> *These I will bring to my holy mountain, and make them joyful in my house of prayer; their burnt offerings and their sacrifices will be accepted on my altar; for my house shall be called a house of prayer for all peoples." Isa 56:7*

One of God's original purposes in building both the tabernacle in the wilderness and then the temple was so that it would be place where man could fellowship with God (Exodus 25:8-9). The temple was a place of communion with God, which by its very nature is prayer. The fact that Isaiah was in the temple tells us that he was in an attitude of prayer, he was seeking God's face.

Prayer points you in the right direction

When Isaiah pursued a prayerful position of humility before God, when Isaiah responded to God's voice with his own voice, it was then that God revealed his calling for Isaiah and gave him clear direction in life. Through prayer Isaiah received instruction on his missionary task. This same principle is true for you and me. If you want to know God's specific will for your life you must seek Him through personal prayer. The heart that prays often and prays passionately is a heart that will gain a new sensitivity to God's leading.

Indecision and anxiety over the decision to go into missions is not something God wants for you. I have heard many young people struggle with the call to missions, they waver between going and staying, and when they do decide to go they are still unsure about the exact location God is sending them to. You don't need to agonize over these choices but you do need to spend time in prayer.

Prayer done correctly is humbling, it is the submission of our will to God's will. Prayer is a deep personal pursuit of God. As we pray we direct our minds and our hearts godward. We may not know the exact next step to take but we know the direction to go, we go to God, always to God. Make your times of prayer regular and make missions an integral part of your prayers and you can be sure God will not leave you without instructions on the next steps of your journey.

I began to pray about my call to missions when I was 16 years old after a missionary visited our church and talked about his work in Togo, Africa. When I started praying about missions I had no idea that God would ever send me to Ukraine. I had a lot of wrong ideas about what I could do and where I would go, however, through prayer God slowly brought my will around and helped me see His plan.

Prayer strengthens your faith

Prayer is to faith what bellows are to a fire. You may have matches, tender and a truckload of firewood, yet without sufficient oxygen your fire will never really take off but rather smolder until it eventually dies out. Prayer blows upon the heart and ignites smoldering logs into blazing flame.

The disciples themselves cried out in prayer to Jesus, "Give us more faith." (Luke 17:5) and the father of the boy who suffered with seizures begged Jesus with tears, "Help my unbelief!" (Mark 9:24) Certainly, God answered these prayers and gave faith. You will also need more faith if you are to go as a missionary. The difficulties that you face now will be increased in a foreign land and culture. Prayer combined with God's Word and meditation are the primary ways of strengthening our faith in God.

Prayer produces right passions

The truth is we tend to pray about the things that mean the most to us. If the gospel and missions has any significance in your life then you will pray about it. This also works the other way; those things we pray about tend to increase in value and significance in our lives.

J.C. Ryle discerningly points out how our prayers reveal our spiritual condition:

"Tell me what a person's prayers are, and I will soon tell you the state of their soul. Prayer is the spiritual pulse. By this the spiritual health may be tested. Prayer is the spiritual weather-glass. By this we may know whether it is fair or foul with our hearts."[11]

1. Do you want to increase your passion for the gospel? Then pray about it!
2. Do you want to increase your passion for the lost? Then pray for them!
3. Do you want to increase your passion for holiness and hatefulness of sin? Then pray about it!
4. Do you want to increase your passion for Christ? Then pray about it!
5. Do you want God to give you divine energy to preach the Good News? The pray about it!

Oh how little we pray for right passions! Sometimes we deceive ourselves thinking that correct Gospel passions will always be there and we neglect to develop them through prayer. It is crucial to deepen those passions now through prayer. You will have times on the mission field when passion will seem lost, when your desire for the gospel will be outweighed by desires of far lesser value. But if you have committed to pray regularly for correct Biblical desires then you will not lose hope but in your discouragement and apathy you will turn to God in prayer and say, "Lord, give me a passion for You and for Your gospel!"

Friend learn to cultivate the habit of praying righteous desires into your life, these prayers will serve you well now and will continue to serve you on the mission field.

Prayer is vital to the mission

Prayer has always played an integral role in God's salvation plan. Jesus spent intense time in prayer before commencing on his great work of salvation (Matthew 26:36). Immediately after Jesus' ascension the

---

11 J.C. Ryle, A Call to Prayer, (Amazon Digital Services, 2011), 44.

first Church turned to God in prayer (Acts 1:14). Those men and women would very soon become powerful missionaries and gospel preachers. When the Church in Jerusalem decided to send out the first missionaries they prayed and fasted (Acts 13:2-3).

We recognize prayer's vital role when we see our inability to complete the task without God's help. Through the act of prayer God gives directions, increases our passion, provides for our needs and begins his salvation work in the lives of others!

How should you prayer about missions in your life? Here are a few suggestions:

1. Pray that God will give you proper preparation.
2. Pray that God will give you immediate opportunity to begin serving and sharing the Gospel.
3. Pray that God would give further clarity as to where he wants you to serve.
4. Pray for other missionaries who are already serving.
5. Pray that God would give you a growing passion for the Gospel and concern for the lost.

Follow up:
1. Can you recall a few times in your own life when God has given you direction in life after you prayed about?
2. Write down 3-4 ways you can be praying about missions over the next 6-12 months.
3. Ask your church and/or several other believer to pray for God's leading in your life.
4. Read A Call to Prayer by J.C. Ryle.

9. Have godly men and women confirmed it?

Christina and I were in Bible college for just one year before we got married. At the time we were both interested in missions but neither of us thought of going to Ukraine. I remember clearly how often people in church who knew us would come up and say,

"So you're going to Ukraine as missionaries right?"

Our response usually went something like this:

"Well, we don't know; we haven't decided yet. It's possible but we are also thinking about some other countries."

Later it turned out that those questions about us going to Ukraine were prophetic. Well, they weren't literally prophecies but the questions came from wise and mature Christians who also knew us well and from a distance could see God's leading in our life better than we could!

If we look at Isaiah we realize that he didn't need the confirmation of others concerning his call to missions, after all he heard the voice of God. Nevertheless I'm sure there were details about his ministry where he sought the counsel of other godly people to help him make wise choices. Most likely you have not received direct revelation from God concerning your call, otherwise you probably wouldn't be reading this book.

It's important that you seek out and pay close attention to the advice of godly men and women around you. Often they can spot certain dangers or possible opportunities that you haven't yet seen. You must realize that the task of missions is not one that you are called to do on your own and thus the confirmation of your call must include others in the Body of Christ.

Without counsel plans fail, but with many advisers they succeed. Pro 15:22

You must seek advice carefully, there are just as many or more texts in Proverbs that warn about those who give bad counsel as there are texts about seeking good counsel. I'd like to share with you a few tips to help you find the right people to get advice from. I suggest that you seriously seek the advice of at least 5-6 different people.

1. **Find someone who has had experience with missions.** May this seems obvious but I think it's important to mention, find at least one counselor who has also experience the call to missions in their personal life. They will be able to share with you about how God called them and how they responded to that call. This kind of experience can be very helpful as you think about how your call may or may not be similar to theirs.

2. **Find someone who knows you well.** Usually those who have known us for 10, 15, or 20 years are the ones who can see our problems the best and are most likely to be honest with us. Most often these are a parent, a sibling, or the pastor of your church.

3. **Find someone who is older than you.** Sometimes it's more comfortable to go to our peers for advice. Certainly you can do this but please don't ignore the older generation. They have wisdom and experiences that you will serve you well.

4. **Find someone in whom you see a passion for God and the Gospel.** When I seek advice always look for someone in whom I see the passions of God. These are passions that I want and I know that their advice will be in line with those passions.

5. **Find someone who has been faithful.** A person who has been faithful in a given ministry over a long period of time is a wise person. If you also would like to become faithful and commit yourself to missions for a lifetime, then you must seek advice from someone who has done the same.

As you're praying about missions, seeking wise counsel, and exploring possibilities, be sure to include your church. One of the most dangerous things a young newly-called missionary can do is to simply go off on his own without the confirmation or blessing of his church. When their first missionaries were sent out from Jerusalem in Acts 13, they were sent by the church. It was not an individual decision but rather church-wide confirmation and sending.

Make sure that you include your own local church early on as you feel that God may be calling you to missions. Talk to your pastor, your small group leader, and other mature Christians in your church. Seek their advice and their approval as you come closer to making your decision. Once you have committed to serving make sure your church takes an active part in sending you to the mission field.

How to receive advice

As you begin to find some people who can give you good advice about missions, let me suggest a few more things that will help you to use that counsel well.

1. **Learn to listen.** First, you should be ready to hear certain truths about yourself that may not be the most pleasant. Your first reaction may be to defend or justify yourself; however, this is exactly what you should not do. Learn to listen carefully and patiently. If you have gone to the right people, then what they are saying certainly has some truth to it.

2. **Review the counsel.** Keep a journal as you listen to advice. One thing you want to be looking for as you talk to different people is common themes. One of those common themes for us was Ukraine! And it turned out that was where God wanted us to go. What topics pop up often in different conversations with different people?

3. **Make a plan.** If your counselors are telling you that they believe God has called you to missions, if they are giving you clear direction and encouraging you to respond to the call, then you must take that counsel and begin to form a plan. You must commit yourself specific actions that will allow you to begin to follow God's call in your life.

Follow up:

1. In your own words, why is it important to include your church as you pursue the call to missions?
2. What are some possible dangers if you don't get good counsel?
3. Make a list of people you can talk to about your desire for missions.

10. Has God given you opportunity?

When God gives a divine desire you can be sure He will also provide an opportunity to fulfill that desire. Our problem is that often we sit and wait for God to give us that one big opportunity and as a result we may miss dozens of smaller opportunities all around us. God uses opportunities to sovereignly orchestrate our lives and he wants us to take advantage of them. You don't have to read much of the Bible before you come across calls to action like, "Work!" "Seek!" "Serve!" "Teach!" and, of course, "Go!"

God doesn't want us sitting on the sidelines waiting for Him to call us on to the field, He's called us all ministry in some form or another. He's also given each of us a position (1 Corinthians 12) and opportunity for ministry that we can begin to take advantage of now. Those who understand this basic principle and get to work in the "little things" will often find more ministry opportunities than they can handle. It is often those who are busiest with ministry that God calls to missions and gives them the opportunity to go.

As a teenager God gave me the desire for missions. I thought I'd like to go to Africa or South America, but before me was the simple opportunity of Ukraine. I had never thought of Ukraine as a place I'd like to go. I hadn't even taken a special interest in Ukraine as a country, and I'm not even sure if I could have correctly place it on the map! Then in one moment Dr. Kempton told me, "There's a great opportunity in Ukraine this summer." God was giving me opportunity that I never asked for. Thankfully, I took it and remained open to God's will.

Ten years later after multiple trips to Ukraine, both my wife and I realized this was the direction God was leading us. We didn't see it right away but as we looked back on all the opportunity over the previous few years, it was hard to deny that God was leading us back to Ukraine.

What does opportunity look like?

Sometimes the reason we miss God-given opportunities is because we are unsure of what they look like. There are times when God gives opportunities in miraculous and special ways. However, in my experience

99 percent of opportunities look exceedly normal, even mundane, and sometimes not very attractive! Yet hidden under the surface of the normal and mundane are often gems of opportunity that will give us unique chances to communicate the Gospel.

1. It must have potential to speak the gospel

When looking for opportunities I suggest starting with the absolute simplest and most basic requirement. A gospel opportunity ought to include the potential of sharing the Gospel. Without this key factor, we have lost our mission focus. The Apostle Paul understood this well and that is why he asked the Church in Colossae to pray that he would have "a door of the Word."

> *Continue steadfastly in prayer, being watchful in it with thanksgiving. At the same time, pray also for us, that God may open to us a door for the word, to declare the mystery of Christ, on account of which I am in prison— that I may make it clear, which is how I ought to speak. Col 4:2-4*

Look around you and take a minute to think about the places you regularly visit. Is there opportunity to share the Gospel hidden under the surface of everyday life? Are there ministry opportunities at your church that would allow you to make contact with unbelievers and share with them the life-giving truth of Jesus Christ? Part of learning to perceive God's leading is cultivating your ability to see those everyday situations of life in light of eternity.

Paul asked others to pray for him concerning these opportunities and we know that God gave Paul plenty of opportunities. Paul traveled to many different cities and countries where he was able to share the gospel as he had opportunity. God even allowed Paul to share the gospel with some of the most powerful rulers of his day. We know that Paul talked with the Ruler Festus and then King Agrippa and his sister Bernice. Later Paul was sent to Rome and while we don't know for sure, it's quite possible that Paul had opportunity to share the message of Jesus with Caesar himself. Caesar was the most powerful man on earth during Paul's time! So, yes, God answered Paul's prayer and gave him opportunity.

2. It may include pain and persecution

However, we must be careful not to forget the methods God used to give Paul opportunity, which were arrest and imprisonment! If you're like me then you don't view legal problems, arrest, and imprisonment as as wonderful opportunities for your ministry but rather as obstacles. We're not the only ones who think that way! Paul's friends also figured that all of these negative things happening to Paul were not good for him and for his ministry.

> And coming to us, he took Paul's belt and bound his own feet and hands and said, "Thus says the Holy Spirit, 'This is how the Jews at Jerusalem will bind the man who owns this belt and deliver him into the hands of the Gentiles.'" When we heard this, we and the people there urged him not to go up to Jerusalem. Then Paul answered, "What are you doing, weeping and breaking my heart? For I am ready not only to be imprisoned but even to die in Jerusalem for the name of the Lord Jesus." And since he would not be persuaded, we ceased and said, "Let the will of the Lord be done." Act 21:11-14

Even Paul's friends didn't view imprisonment as an opportunity for Paul and begged him not to go. Paul went anyway, and just as was prophesied he did end up in prison, but it was that very fact that allowed him to speak to some the most influential people of his day. Later on Paul writes to his friends in Philippi and tells them:

> I want you to know, brothers, that what has happened to me has really served to advance the gospel, so that it has become known throughout the whole imperial guard and to all the rest that my imprisonment is for Christ. And most of the brothers, having become confident in the Lord by my imprisonment, are much more bold to speak the word without fear. Php 1:12-14

Paul saw the opportunity in his imprisonment not only to speak to the rulers of his day but also to share the gospel with the guards and possibly other prisoners as well. We must be careful not to look for opportunity only in comfortable, convenient, and conventional looking places because often opportunity comes knocking in the form of problems, pain, and prison!

3. It should have signs of positive faith responses

Looking at Paul's missionary journeys we see a pattern of ministry choice. Paul goes and remains longer in those places that had some sort of positive response to the Gospel. When Paul and Barnabas returned from their missionary trip to Antioch and Syria they share with the church in Jerusalem the following:

> *And when they arrived and gathered the church together, they declared all that God had done with them, and how he had opened a door of faith to the Gentiles. (Act 14:27)*

It appears that God not only gave them the ability to travel and the opportunity to preach the gospel but he also gave them real faith responses. Paul calls it "a door of faith to the nations." As you think about possible missions opportunities or even simple opportunities to share the gospel it makes sense to focus on those opportunities that are showing signs of true faith in response to your preaching of the gospel. This is not only wise but also another way in which you can become sensitive to God's leading in your life.

Of course I don't want to discredit ministries that have labored long with few visible results. We talked about the danger of evaluating the success of our ministry based upon the numbers that have responded under question #7, "Do you understand the task before you?"

Looking for signs of true faith responses isn't exactly the same as evaluating your ministry by the numbers of people who show up. Sometimes it may only be just one or two or a handful of people who respond positively. These responses are from God and when present they require us to give them our attention, to make sure they are growing in the faith and it is wise to continue preaching the gospel in that area or with that group of people because we have already seen that God is at work.

4. It should be flexible

Finally we must view all opportunities as temporary openings for the Gospel, staying flexible and ready for new opportunities. Look how Paul writes to the Corinthian Church about his ministry in Ephesus.

I will visit you after passing through Macedonia, for I intend to pass through Macedonia, and perhaps I will stay with you or even spend the winter, so that you may help me on my journey, wherever I go. For I do not want to see you now just in passing. I hope to spend some time with you, if the Lord permits. But I will stay in Ephesus until Pentecost, for a wide door for effective work has opened to me, and there are many adversaries. (1Co 16:5-9)

Paul wasn't rigidly nailed down to one place or even one ministry method. He stayed open to God's leading and when he sensed good gospel opportunity he maximized it by focusing his time and efforts upon that area where he saw God working. Our main task in missions isn't to establish a lasting organization but rather to preach an everlasting gospel to whomever will listen. When we focus on this main task of missions we may find that opportunities take us to places that we would have never thought of on our own.

If you are seriously thinking about missions it's likely that you already have an opportunity or two and you are going with those opportunities in mind. That is good and it is most likely God's leading in your life. Yet, I encourage you not to hold those opportunities too tightly. You may find that things look much different than you had expected once you arrive on the field. You may find that those opportunities that brought you to the field in the first place no longer exists. These kinds of revelations can be discouraging and that's why it's so important to be flexible and understand that no opportunity is eternal.

If you find that an opportunity isn't what you expected or no longer exists, don't let that discourage you. God brought you to where you are for a reason. It could be that the initial opportunity was just a stepping stone to some greater opportunity. Look around and I'm sure you'll find that God has some other opportunities that are just as great or greater for gospel impact.

Follow up:

1. How would you define a "Gospel opportunity?"
2. What are some ways God has already used a painful experience in your life as a Gospel opportunity?
3. Can you already name a few Gospel opportunities that God has given you? Write them down.
4. Take some time to pray over the possible opportunities you have written down.

11. How did you answer the questions?

Let's quickly review the 10 questions in this section of the book.

1. Are you in the right place?
2. Do you understand the holiness of God?
3. Do you understand the wretched nature of sin?
4. Has God prepared you?
5. Do you understand the nature of the call?
6. Do you have a desire to go?
7. Do you understand the task before you?
8. Have you prayed about it?
9. Have godly men and women confirmed it?
10. Has God given you opportunity?

I encourage you not to quickly answer these questions but rather to study them and give careful thought to each one. Make each question a matter of prayer and ask God for guidance as you seek His will.

These questions are in no way a scientific means of determining your calling, nor are they a "Gideon's fleece." Except for in the rare case of a few prophets God does not give us verbal instructions that are specific to our personal call. He expects us to use principles of wisdom, planning, prayer, and council. Our task in navigating His will is to be open and sensitive to His leading. Part of how we do that is through careful study and thoughtful analysis of our own lives. Asking yourself the questions in this book can be part of that process. I believe that if you approach these questions with a humble and sincere desire to know God's will for your life you will likely come away with a clearer picture of God's leading.

If after careful study, prayer, and counsel with other mature believers you find that all your answers are "Yes" then I think it's fair to say that there is high possibility that God is calling you to missions! I also believe it's fair to say that it would probably be sin for you to further ignore that call in your life. It would be a mistake if you didn't at least take a few more steps of faith forward towards missions. Go on a short-term trip, talk to some missionaries who are on the field about your desire, investigate possible mission organizations that you could work with. These are all steps you seriously need to think about taking in the immediate future.

Follow up:
1. Ask God what steps He wants you to take next.
2. Write down a few actions steps that you could begin to work on immediately.
3. Call your spiritual mentor or pastor and discuss these actions steps with him.

Answers to Common Questions

Once you've recognized your own call to missions, the practical questions start coming. Many of them from well-meaning family members, which is where we'll start because family issues are one of the biggest factors for missionaries. Family issues don't just bring missionaries home but they often play a large factor in determining where they will minister and in what particular ministry they will be involved.

How does marriage affect my call?

I'm not sure I can think of anything that can have such a great impact on your life and your ability to serve as a missionary as marriage. Many young people simply "fall in love" and do not think much about how their future spouse may affect their call to missions. If God is calling you to do His work in a far-off land then it makes sense to look at your life as a whole and make sure you are not creating barriers to what God has called you to do. Marriage can either be a barrier to missions or a great benefit so you must be very careful.

This section however, is not only for singles who are considering missions and marriage but also for those of you who are already married and thinking about missions. It is my firm belief that God never calls one spouse to missions without calling the other spouse. This is a decision you'll need to make together, it is a step of faith that must be synchronized as you move forward. The mission field can be a dangerous place for marriages. Unless you are fully committed to each other, to God, and to the mission you can easily fall into trouble.

Marriage will make you busier

Very simply put, a man or a woman who is married doesn't have as much time for ministry as someone who is single. This may not seem very significant but it really is an important truth to keep in mind.

Notice what Paul says:

I want you to be free from anxieties. The unmarried man is anxious about the things of the Lord, how to please the Lord. But the married man is anxious about worldly things, how to please his wife. (1Co 7:32-33)

Paul does not say you shouldn't get married but he does mention that marriage means you are now required to care for another person. If you are single you have much more time for ministry that a married person does. This is also important for married people to remember. Too many men forget that they are married once they get on the mission field and fail to care for their wives. This can have disastrous results in the long-run if they don't modify their schedules. If you're married then your primary responsibility is first to your spouse and family and then to your ministry. If more missionaries could follow that simple order we'd see a lot more missionary families stay on the field longer.

Marriage may keep you from ever getting to field

On several occasions I have talked with young people who were excited about missions. With passion these young men and women described the desire God had given them to serve. Many of them had already gotten their feet wet in missions through short term trips and now they were ready to make a commitment for the long-haul.

Then something happened that they may not have exactly thought through: they fell in love. Their new-found love was not as excited about missions as they were, they may not have been outright against it but they were not burning with passion. Many of these young people hoped that over time God would give their future spouse that same desire and passion for missions that He had given them. Unfortunately, I can't think of one time where that was the case. In every situation I've seen, the spouse who felt called to missions eventually let go of the hope of ever serving God on the foreign field.

Friend, if you believe God has called you to missions you must approach all of life with that calling in mind. Marriage and love are not exceptions to your calling! Often young people are intentional about planning out their future in regards to their chosen profession or ministry but when it comes to love they just let it happen to them. You must also take an intentional approach to love and marriage. Make sure you are directed by Scriptural principles of wisdom rather than just falling emotionally for any boy or girl who manages to stir-up your hormones. What I'm saying is that if God is calling you to missions and you're single now, then you should take every measure to make sure that if you are to "fall in love" it will be with a man or woman who shares the same calling as you!

One of the simplest ways you can do this is by developing relationships with others who are also pursuing God and pursuing missions. Do your best to surround yourself with these kind of people and there will be much less of a chance that you will "fall in love" with someone who doesn't share your passion or calling. For me this meant going to Bible college. While not everyone was pursuing missions there, most were pursuing ministry and some were pursuing missions. Early on in my relationship with Christina we shared with each other how we felt God was calling us and clearly God had called us both to missions!

Before you begin a romantic relationship learn what goals and aspirations he or she has. If their calling and passions look similar to yours then that may be a good sign that this person is right for you. However, if he or she is not called to missions, or it's evident that they don't really share your passion for missions then be careful not to develop a romantic emotional attachment that could be hard to break.

Marriage may take you off the field

Another situation I have seen is when one spouse is much more zealous about missions than the other spouse. Sometimes this can happen because one spouse convinced the other to go to the mission field despite his or her reservations. Although they may have technically agreed upon it, eventually it becomes evident that one spouse has the passion and the other not so much. This can lead to significant friction in marriage and often can result in the couple coming home sooner than expected.

If you and your spouse lack unity and are not in complete agreement about your call to missions then you are in the danger zone! What can you do if you find yourself in this situation?

1. Don't overlook the problem.

Making missions or ministry a higher priority than your spouse is one of the worst things you can do. Doing that makes it easy to ignore possible signs that he or she may not completely share your passion or calling.

Ask yourself some questions:
1. How does your spouse respond when you talk with him/her about the mission?

2. What kind of interest does he/she express in the conversation?
3. Does your spouse bring up the topic themselves or are you the only one who brings it up?
4. Does your spouse often complain about how busy you are with ministry?
5. Do you sense regret or bitterness in your spouse because of your mission?

Certainly all of these types of things could come up in the normal daily struggles of life; however, if you are hearing or seeing some of these things on a regular basis then you need to take note and not simply ignore the problem.

2. Never manipulate or guilt trip your spouse into ministry.

Most of us wouldn't intentionally manipulate our spouse into missions. However, this can happen even unintentionally when we resort to methods of guilt tripping in order to get our spouse to agree to a certain ministry or even to become missionaries. Unfortunately this method will almost always end disastrously.

If you have to win an argument in order to get your spouse to agree to missions, then you haven't really won anything at all except the dismay of your spouse. If you have to guilt trip your spouse by comparing them to "so and so" and their amazing ministry then you are also going down the wrong road.

A lack of passion or desire for mission can never be changed through manipulation and guilt trips; it must be changed at the heart level. If you notice that your spouse lacks this desire then I suggest that you start by making this a regular matter of prayer. Pray that God will give your spouse an unquenchable thirst for God Himself and then for God's mission. Let God be the change agent.

Let's not forget that it's very possible that your spouse's lack of desire for missions may be a direct result of a problem he or she sees in your own life. Stop and take a look at yourself, how are you treating your spouse? Are you being hypocritical in anyway? Does your spouse see an inconsistency in how you are in ministry setting as opposed to how you are at home? Does your spouse feel that he or she has to compete with the ministry for your favor and attention?

These and other problems can be big turn offs to missions for your spouse.

3. Make your spouse your first mission.

Above all you need to be keenly aware and concerned for your spouse's spiritual condition. Are you praying regularly, deeply, and passionately for your husband or wife? Does your spouse sense that your priority is his/her physical, emotional, and spiritual welfare?

What are you doing to ensure your spouse is flourishing spiritually? Are you reading God's Word together, are you praying together, are you daily asking questions about how they are doing spiritually and how you can help or encourage them? Are you allowing them to have time each day to personally focus on Bible reading and prayer?

Ultimately, your desire ought to be that your husband or wife have the closest possible relationship with God. If this happens then you can forget about problems with passion concerning the mission, they will probably be a step ahead of you!

4. Cultivate a gospel awareness in your marriage.

Finally, you must consciously and consistently cultivate gospel awareness in your own marriage. Make your marriage an oasis of Gospel, grace, and truth. Be frequent in prayer with your spouse; practice prompt forgiveness and patient mercy. Let you marriage marinate in the flavors of grace, mercy, kindness, and devotion. Find time to read and study God's Word together. Find time to pray for each other privately. Find time to share your struggles and allow each other to speak Gospel truth into your lives. Learn to worship Christ daily with your spouse. Try to find ways that you can serve each other and ways that you can serve others together. Don't just talk about the "how" of missions but talk about the "why" of missions.

These are not things to do in preparation for the mission field but rather they are vital elements of a Christ centered marriage that will help you go to the mission field with a spiritually healthy marriage and stay on that field with a marriage that grows in faith and deepens in love and passion not only for each other but also for Jesus Christ! This must be the highest goal of your marriage!

Strong marriages make strong missionaries.

While I have seen people never get to the field or have to leave the field because of a weak marriage, I have also seen the power of a strong marriage on the field. All forms of ministry have a tendency to drain you spiritually, emotionally, and sometimes even physically. Couples who have a strong marriage built on the Biblical foundations of mutual love, respect, and understanding find that their marriage is a refuge from the spiritual drain of ministry. It is the place they go often to find spiritual, emotional, and physical refreshment. In a good marriage both husband and wife know how to encourage each other, how to help to other relieve his/her burdens, and how to minister to their needs--mutual and individual. In marriages where this kind of mutual interaction and help is present you will find some of the greatest missionaries.

Learn to serve and minister to your spouse before learning to serve and minister to those outside of your marriage. If you and your spouse can do this one simple thing you will set yourselves up for future ministry that will be lasting and will open up opportunities that you never thought possible.

What if my parents are against it?

Occasionally one or both parents will be against their child going to the mission field. These situations need careful thought and prayer. Sometimes the concerns come from unbelieving parents who do not understand the mission and thus can't comprehend the need to go. On the other hand these concerns can come from believing parents, sometimes for valid reasons and sometimes for not so valid reasons.

If your parents are opposed to you going to the mission field you must not automatically think that their opposition is motivated by unbiblical presuppositions, most likely there is at least a grain of truth to their resistance. It is vital that you take time to seriously investigate their concerns.

Be respectful

No matter how silly or unbiblical your parents concerns may seem, you must approach the matter with all respect and honor for your parents. Keep in mind the 5th commandment "Honor your father and mother" (Exodus 20:12). This commandment was given to mainly to adult children. It did not imply blind obedience to absolutely everything the parents say but rather a humble attitude of respect and honor. It may have even implied the idea of caring for elderly parents.

Sometimes it can be difficult to have a level of respect for parents who don't live respectable lives and who don't understand your love for Jesus. However, the fifth commandment isn't given only to those children with believing parents but to all children no matter how their parents believe.

If you sense that your parents will be against you going to the mission field, I encourage you to spend deep time in prayer before talking to them. Ask God to help you have a humble and respectful spirit. When you do have a chance to talk with them try to stay away from arguments and quarrelling. Assure them of your love for them, assure them that you don't want to disappoint them or be disrespectful of them.

Approach this matter with a great deal of respect and it is much more likely that eventually your parents will come around. Approaching this matter aggressively, ready to debate and show them who's right will only further cement their already negative presuppositions.

Listen to their concerns

Part of honoring your parents is learning to simply listen to their concerns. Their concerns may be unfounded, they may sound preposterous, they may even be irrational but you need to give them the respect of quietly listening to them and allowing them to express their concerns.

On the other hand, your parents probably know you quite well. They may even know you better than you think. So, it's quite likely that their concerns may have some substance to them. As you prepare to listen to their concerns don't let yourself automatically assume that their worries are baseless or trite.

In question #9 we talked about the importance of getting the advice of godly men and women who know you well. Even if your parents are not godly, they most likely know you well, so listen carefully, you may find that the issues they bring up really do need to be attended to you.

Consider taking time to sit down with your parents just to listen to their concerns. Ask them why they don't want you to go, let them explain and then ask further questions so that you have a better understanding.

1. Do they fear for your safety?
2. Do they just think it's an unwise career move for you?
3. Do they feel like you or their grandkids will be too far from them?
4. Do they think you've become some sort of fanatical follower of Jesus?

Help your parents more clearly describe their worries and opposition to you going to the mission field. Do it without debate or counter arguments. Let them know how thankful you are for their parental concern and care. Write down the specific issues that your parents mentioned and promise them that you will give these issues serious consideration and prayer and that you'll respond to them later.

Respond to their opposition

Responding to your parents' opposition must be done only after carefully and respectfully listening to their concerns, taking time to consider the issues they raised, and prayerfully asking God for wisdom and guidance in this matter. In addition to these I also suggest that you talk with the same godly men and women with whom you sought advice as I we talked about in question #9.

After carefully considering their concerns there may be several conclusions that you come to.

1. You may find that, indeed their concerns are well founded and you probably shouldn't go to the mission field, at least not anytime soon.
2. You may find that they raise some issues that should be addressed in your life before leaving for the mission field.
3. You may find that their concerns are based on misinformation and they just need to be correctly informed.
4. You may find that their concerns are based on a difference in core beliefs.

No matter what conclusion you come to you will need to respond to your parents and let them know what course of action you have decided to take after considering their concerns. Once again be careful to do this in a respectful manner. Consider writing out the issues they brought up and writing out your response, this can help you more accurately communicate and sometimes helps when there are strong emotions involved.

Assure them of your love and respect

Finally, throughout this process make sure you constantly assure your parents of your love and respect for them. Let them know that you want to stay in touch with them while you're on the mission field, invite them to visit you if they have opportunity. Try your best to keep an open line of communication.

How do children affect my call?

The question of children weighs upon the heart of every parent. We want our our kids to be safe, have a good education, and to enjoy their young years. Children take a significant amount of time, care, and money! How will they affect the mission? How will they react to moving to a foreign country or a different city? What will they think of leaving their friends behind? How will they feel when they become the minority?

Remember they weren't called

While I do not believe God ever calls one spouse without calling the other the same can not be said for children. Your children go to the mission field because you are going. Sometimes they may not even be asked their opinion about this move. They may not want to go, they may have great fears about going, they may not understand why they are going but they go because they are part of the family.

On one hand that can sound somewhat negative but on the other hand I know plenty of missionary kids who are very grateful that they live in a foreign country and wouldn't want it any other way! The important thing here is that as parents you realize that your children will have a significantly different perspective on the mission than you have. For you the mission field may seem exciting, God has probably already given you a passion for the people to whom you are going, you have likely already communicated with people on the field, maybe you have already made a short trip or two. You are somewhat familiar with how things will be and what you will be doing. However, don't forget that your children will know far less about this new place than you. They will have much more difficulty comprehending what it will be like in a new country and culture.

Include them in the process

As soon as your children are old enough it's important that you communicate with them regularly about your plans to go to the mission field. While it's not necessarily their decision to make, they should be included as much as possible, especially as you make decisions about schooling and things that will more directly affect them.

My wife and I have four children. When we left for the mission field they were 8, 6, 2, and 8 months old. Our oldest two had traveled with us to Ukraine before so they knew a little of what life would be like there and they were excited to go. We often talked with them about what we would be doing in Ukraine, and why we were going. I believe this communication was important to their understanding and the played a role in their anticipation.

Communicate your passions

Telling your children what the mission field will be like is one thing but as parents we must do much more. As we talked with our children we also communicated our own excitement to be part of God's work. We tried to explain to them the spiritual needs which were the real reason why we were going.

In my experience there's often one significant factor between children who adjust well and enjoy life on the mission field and those who don't: the attitude of the parents towards the country and culture where they are living. Unfortunately negative attitudes are much more easily caught than positive ones. So if you are very apprehensive about the mission, if you are unsure and worried, if you develop a bitterness towards the nationals, if you often complain about the way things are done in your new country, then you can be sure your children will pick up on these things and echo them.

For your children's sake, it's vital to keep the mission at the forefront of your thinking. Remember your task, remember your calling, remember your primary mission to tell the Good News to a dying world. If you lose sight of your purpose and your calling, your children will not understand why you are going to the mission field and why you must stay. The more you develop a passion for telling the Good News and a love for the people whom you are serving, the less you will be tempted to complain or struggle with bitterness in your new culture.

Remember the unique pressures of missions

The unique pressures of the mission field begin before you get to your chosen place of ministry. I remember well the months we spent visiting churches and raising support. These were tough times for the family. We were often on the road, often guests staying with people we had just met. Nearly every Sunday our children were introduced to inquisitive crowds of unfamiliar people. Missionary kids are expected to behave better than the average kid, but it doesn't always turn out that way. Constant travel can be draining on adults and children alike.

As you prepare for the mission field I encourage you to try to place yourself in your children's shoes. What may seem simple and easy for you may be extremely difficult and confusing for them. If your support raising includes traveling I encourage you to often take time just for your family. Go out of your way to visit a zoo or an attraction along the road just with your family. Your children will appreciate the time when they can be themselves without the pressures of "performing" for a new crowd.

Once you're on the mission field it's also important to recognize your children's experience will be far different from yours. Depending on your setting and often on your schooling arrangement your children may take on the new language and culture much faster than you. Each child will respond differently to the new setting. Some may find it easy to acquire the new way of life and some more difficult. It's important that you are sensitive to the particular needs of each child.

No matter how your child accepts the new culture you must understand that he will never quite be a "native" nor will he completely remain the culture in which he was raised. You children will have a third culture that will be a unique mix of the the two cultures. For them going "home" for furlough won't exactly be going "home." The simple question, "Where are you from?" will not have a simple answer.

Missionary kids are unique and they deserve our unique attention. Our family has found it extremely important that our kids develop friendships on the field as well as friendships with other missionary kids. Other missionary kids understand each other in ways that missionary parents don't. As you have opportunity look for ways that you children can develop both relationships with nationals and with other missionary kids.

Include them in the mission

Including your child in the mission is vital but it must be done with wisdom and balance. Do what you can to make your child a part of the mission but don't make them do missions. What I'm saying is that you really need wisdom and balance here. Forcing your child to to fill the gap when there's not enough volunteers could result in bitterness in your child. Sometimes there's a fine line between getting your child involved and forcing them to participate even though they lack desire to do so themselves. Your children can be extremely helpful but they shouldn't be looked at as an ever-ready volunteer bank for your ministry.

That being said I believe there is a proper place to involve your children. In my observation of many missionary families I have noticed that in those families where there is ministry involvement the children often will have a positive experience and will often end up in missions or ministry themselves.

Of course there are more benefits than just giving a positive experience. Being involved in your ministry offers an excellent way to disciple and train your child spiritually, in addition their involvement is a real ministry and blessing to others. As much as possible look for ways for your family to be involved in the ministry. Also remember that as your children get older they may be interested in getting involved in ministries that you are not directly a part of your main ministry. This independence can be a very healthy way for them to serve in a way that matches the gifting God has given them.

Disciple them

Finally I want to encourage you to intentionally, regularly, prayerfully, and lovingly disciple your children throughout the process of becoming missionaries and being missionaries. Unfortunately, often there is an unsaid expectation that missionaries are "spiritual giants" and since their children are also the offspring of "spiritual giants" then they must be "spiritual giants" in the making.

In general the parents of missionary kids know better, after all all they see their children day in and day out and they have to deal with the unpleasant results of sin in their own lives and in the lives of their children. Nevertheless it seems that some of those assumptions about the spiritual health and well-being of missionary kids has rubbed off on missionary parents. Maybe we think that since we are taking care of the spiritual needs of others then God will certainly take care of our children's spiritual needs. Maybe we think that if we personally have a close walk with God then our children will also. Maybe we think that a good homeschooling program or Sunday school will meet their spiritual needs.

These assumptions sometimes go unsaid, but they too often represent the way missionary parents raise their children. When it comes to questions of faith, repentance, and spiritual growth we must never be so naive as to make such assumptions. Becoming a missionary yourself in no way guarantees that you children are automatically on the right path. They need your time and your special attention to their spiritual development. You must labor with them in discipleship, you must take the time to personally communicate the truths of God's Word into their lives. You must work hard to establish a loving and trusting relationship with them that will allow you guide them precisely and along the path of faith.

Just as your marriage can have a direct and serious effect on your mission, so also can your children! Neglect the spiritual condition of your children and sooner or later they will take you off the field. Conversely children who are experience the careful and loving spiritual guidance of their parents can often be a huge benefit to the ministry.

Do I need to go to Bible college or seminary?

I entered Bible college fall of 1996 and graduated from seminary in spring of 2005. That's nine years of life that I mainly devoted to formal Bible and ministry training. I know that to some that sounds like an awful lot of time, and believe me, it sounded like a lot to me when I was in the middle of those years. However, something kept me going. Maybe it was the realization that I just wasn't quite ready yet, maybe it was fact that I really needed more time to mature, maybe it was the understanding that without a strong Biblical foundation I wouldn't do much good on the mission field and possibly could do a lot of harm!

There were times during those nine years when I would have loved to just "run away" to the mission field. There were times when I felt like I was spinning my wheels, wasting my time, and not fulfilling my calling. God gave me the desire to serve Him so why couldn't I go immediately and start that service?

Yes, there were times when I doubted the need for all that study and preparation. Yet, now I as I write this, 12 years after graduating from seminary, I can tell without any doubt that those nine years were not wasted. I can tell you that if I had to do it all over again, I'd do it exactly the same way. I can tell you that I'm very grateful for those years of preparation and I see now how God used them to develop me spiritually, doctrinally, and professionally.

That was my experience, but what about you? Do you really need to go to Bible college or seminary? In short my answer is this:

Formal Bible training is optional; serious Bible study and preparation is not!

No matter who you are, no matter what your age, no matter the specifics of the ministry you'll be involved in, you need serious training and preparation! You need to learn to study God's Word personally, systematically, and skillfully. You need to develop a strong base in core Bible doctrines, you need to learn essential ministry skills. All of these are a must if you want to be a successful missionary. Whether or not you choose to learn these things through a more formal course of study or not is up to you.

While formal Bible and ministry training isn't mandatory for missions I do believe it should be seriously considered. I have only met a handful of ministers and mission leaders who had no formal training and were successful. Those were men and women of exceptional talent, extreme discipline, and extraordinary minds. They may not have attended a formal Bible school, but they studied hard throughout their ministries and proved themselves able students of the Word.

In today's world formal training programs are much more accessible than they were even 30 years ago. So what I'm saying is, if you have the option, I highly recommend that you at least give formal training a shot. Let me first give you several reasons why it might be important for you to enter a solid Biblical and ministry training program. Then I'll talk a little bit about why you might instead choose an informal method of preparation for missions.

Why should you get formal training?

1. It will give you a broader base.
Generally formal training will help you to broaden your base of knowledge more than informal studies. Formal education gives you a range of teachers who will introduce you to more diverse theologies and systems of thought then you would find if you were on your own. This is vital, especially when going to a foreign culture. You must learn to identify and think in systems that are not native to you. For most people this is an uncomfortable task. Formal education helps give you the push and stretch you need in order to tackle difficult and before unthought of issues in Scripture and in ministry.

You can be sure that once you arrive on the mission field you will be greeted by many more foreign theological and ministry related issues. If this is your first time meeting such problems, you may not be very successful in thinking through them and determining a Biblical course of action. Having a broad base of experienced teachers can make the difference of success or failure.

2. It will help you stay disciplined.

While I've met some people who thought they had the discipline to train themselves I've met fewer people who actually possessed that discipline. We often tend to think of ourselves as more disciplined than reality proves. It's fairly easy to set a course of study, write out the list of books to read, papers to write, and put it all down on the calendar. It's a 1,000 times harder to carry that plan out to the end!

The clear boundaries, grading system, and accountability of formal education help us stay disciplined. Sometimes it's even the money that we pay for schooling that helps stay to course. If you're like me then you need that discipline.

3. It has proven standards of education.

I understand that there are many different schools out there and you must be careful to pick one that will offer you a proven standard of education. However, generally speaking schools follow standards that have developed over years of experience and tens of thousands of hours of instruction and training. There's wisdom in that experience that comes out in how the program is build, what classes are offered, and the types of work you're required to do.

4. It will make you more accepted in some cultures.

Where will you be serving as a missionary? For some countries and cultures it's very important to have a formal education. While both you and I understand that a degree on paper may in reality say little about your readiness to serve, it can however open up many more opportunities for you once you get to the mission field. Look into the culture and find out if it would make a big difference whether or not you had a degree. Many Eastern cultures highly value formal education and a degree in your hand can open the doors to many ministry opportunities.

5. It can allow you to formally teach.

Finally, a formal training program will allow you to teach formally. Often missionaries are involved in teaching in Bible schools and seminaries. Additionally, they may sometimes teach in secular schools. If you are going to be formally teaching then you'll want to get a formal education.

What about informal training?

Depending upon your ministry and current situation it may be difficult or time may not allow you to get a formal training. Informal training can be helpful when you need a more flexible approach or if you don't have the funds to pay for schooling. One advantage informal training has over formal training is that it can be tailored to meet your exact needs.

1. Find a competent mentor.

Informal training doesn't mean "solo" training. If you want to give yourself the best possible preparation you'll need to find a good mentor. When looking for a mentor I suggested you review the points I gave in question #9 about seeking godly counsel. This is the kind of person you should be looking for in a mentor.

The mentor's task is to give you general guidance through the process of your studies, encourage you, give you helpful advice, pray for you and keep you accountable. This is not an easy task and it may be difficult to find someone willing to take it on. While it's ideal to have one person who would help you with all these things you may find that it will be easier to have 2-3 mentors who can help you with different aspects of your training.

As much as possible include your own pastor in this process and your local church. Your pastor may or may not be your mentor but he should be informed of your progress and have a general idea of what you are studying. This connection helps keep you accountable on the local church level, which will be vital later as you go to the mission field.

2. Look at what schools are doing

Take time to look at training programs of some schools that have produce Biblically sound and successful missionaries and ministry leaders. What courses are in their program? What textbooks are they using? What kind of assignments are they requiring? What other books are they reading? Asking these questions may help you determine what topics you should focus on, what material to use, and what kind of assignments will be most helpful.

Several schools also have video lectures available for free. You might find these to be a helpful resource to your studies.

3. Read

There can be no real learning without reading. The Apostle Paul knew that and that is why he asked Timothy to bring him his books (2 Timothy 4:13). Even if you feel like reading is not your "thing" you must find the time and discipline to read. Spurgeon said it well:

> *"Give yourself unto reading. The man who never reads will never be read; he who never quotes will never be quoted. He who will not use the thoughts of other men's brains, proves that he has no brains of his own. You need to read."* [12]

The point in reading isn't to get through as many books as possible but rather to spur your mind on to think about things in new and helpful ways. Your reading should aid you in your ability to think about the Bible, theology, and how those truths connect to real life. Your reading should not only help you better understand Biblical truth but should encourage and exhort you to apply Biblical truth personally.

Here are a few helpful suggestions to guide your reading:

A. Focus on the classics

While there are many new and popular books coming out all the time it's my conviction that there is never anything completely new said. For that reason I believe it is wise to focus on reading classic books, especially early on in your education. Of course, you don't want to completely ignore newer books, sometimes they can be helpful in understanding the Biblical position on contemporary issues that did not exists 100 years ago. Nevertheless, avoid the temptation to grab every popular new book that finds its place onto the bookstore shelf.

---

12 C.H. Spurgeon, "Paul—His Cloak and His Books," Sermon no. 542

B. Read theologies

Make sure you include several good theologies in your reading list. These will help you piece together the teachings of Scripture on some of the most foundational issues.

C. Read deeply

Read with a highlighter and a pen. Record your thoughts, write your responses. Take time to look up the passages. Work with the text, struggle with the text, allow your mind to engage.

D. Read broadly

Read a wide range of authors and types of books. You don't want to only read theologies nor do you want to exclusively read "how to books." Try to find a balance between theology, practice, exhortation, and church history. I can also be helpful at times to read authors that may not be exactly within your strain of theology. This will help you better understand your own theology.

E. Read consistently

Develop a reading plan for yourself to help you read consistently. Make sure you talk it over with your mentor and ask him to help keep you accountable in your reading.

4. Write

Reading and writing are two sides of one coin. Just as reading will force you to think on aspects of theology that you had not entered your mind before, so writing will force you to become clear and concise in your thoughts about those new issues.

Talk with your mentor about possible writing projects, these may include book reviews, research projects, textual issues, and others.

5. Minister

Finally, make sure you are getting practical experience in ministry in your local church. One of the worst things you can do is go to the mission field with little or no practical ministry experience. You can be sure that on the mission field you will face ministry issues that you have never faced at home. Nevertheless people are people and sin is sin, so many of the issues you face will be similar. Thus every moment of ministry experience that you can find at home will only serve to multiply your effectiveness on the field.

Do I need a mission agency?

The short answer is, "no" you don't need a mission agency but don't go running off to a foreign country by yourself just yet. While a mission agency isn't a Biblical requirement for missionaries, it is often a wise decision. If you do choose to go without a mission agency that doesn't mean you should be a "lone ranger." You still need a sending structure and a support system. This is not a task you should be doing all on your own.

In this section we will look at the benefits of going with a more traditional mission agency and the benefits of going with a smaller more informal sending structure.

Benefits of a mission agency

While mission agency differ greatly from one organization to the other in general I see four primary benefits of going with a missions agency. These they include: Team, experience, finances, and accountability.

1. Team

More often than not a mission agency will give you opportunity to work with a team of other missionaries some of whom may have many years of experience on the field where you are headed to. Team ministry can be a huge benefit to you in several different ways. In the early stages of your new life on the field it means you'll have others who can help you get settled in your new country, who can acquaint you with your surroundings and give you good advice. As you get into more ministry a team means a broader base of contacts with national churches and believers. It allows for more opportunity to work together on large ministry projects, and it means more collective wisdom in the planning of these projects. Teams can also be a great help in covering ministry responsibilities when you go on furlough. Finally teams can just be an encouragement to you and your family as they provide personal fellowship, a listening ear, and someone near who can pray for you and with you.

Honestly, it's not always easier to with with a team. Certainly interpersonal relationships can be difficult and tension can result as a result of disagreements over ministry choices and even personal choices. Some prefer to work on their own in order to avoid the problems of working with a team. While working alone can be "easier" it that doesn't mean it is better or more effective.

2. Experience

There are many potential pitfalls in missions that could be disastrous. These unforeseen problems can be anything from sexual temptations, to burnout, to financial problems. Mission agencies usually carry with them the collective wisdom of working with dozens if not hundreds or thousands of missionaries. This means that often the mission agency will have policies in place and people with experience available to help you navigate potential problems that you may not be able to foresee on your own.

3. Accountability

We may not like to admit it but we all need some form of accountability. A mission agency makes it easier to have a system of accountability in place. If you have a team on your field then you already have some built in accountability. Usually the mission will also have some sort of regional accountability in place. These structures help make sure you don't get "lost" on the mission field. If your nearest accountability is 4,000 miles away, let's just say, that's not the best scenario! Having someone closer to you with holding you in regular accountability concerning yourself, your family, and your ministry is a great benefit.

4. Finances

Finances will play a significant role in your missionary service and quite frankly they can be a real headache! Mission agencies are usually able to significantly reduce that headache for their missionaries by receiving, processing, and tracking donations. Also they generally take care of things like making sure the proper taxes get payed, that you have some sort of retirement, health insurance, and many other details related to finances. By doing this they not only make your life easier but they also allow you to have more time to dedicate to ministry on your field.

Benefits of informal sending structure

I think it's safe to say that over the history of the Church most missionaries were not sent out by traditional mission agencies. The Church has a long history of sending its missionaries out through structures set up either in one local church or through the common effort of several churches. Even today in much of the Eastern world many if not most missionaries are still being sent by informal sending structures.

An informal sending structure should have close ties with your sending church. Often it is the missionary's local church but not always. It should also have some ability to provide you with accountability both spiritually and financially. Finally it should be interested in your success and ready to actively pray for you work to make sure you are supported. It is also important that you keep in regular communication with them.

The benefits of having an informal sending and support structure is that it often allows you to move much quicker. It generally won't have high and complicated organizational structures which means decisions about ministry can be processed much quicker. Generally the personal investment in you is higher as well and overhead operational costs are lower, which means you won't need to raise as much funds for support.

Either way you go, make sure you have a good team who can support you, pray for you, and provide accountability.

What if I can't raise the support I need?

Raising support can be a long, frustrating, and, at times, discouraging process. Many prospective missionaries view raising support as a "necessary evil" that unfortunately must be taken care of in order for a missionary to get to the field. Some missionaries start off well but after years of trying still don't have all the support their mission agency requires and they end up never reaching their desired field. What should you do if you find yourself in this situation? Should you give up? Should you look for other options? Is this just another hurdle to jump over?

First, let me say that what I'm writing here should not be viewed in any way as a fundraising "how to," there are plenty of books and training seminars on that topic. Instead let me help you form a balanced perspective and healthy Biblical attitude about fundraising and even share a few steps to make sure you're on the right track.

Let's start by looking at a few unhelpful attitudes and how we can change them.

1. Fundraising is a necessary evil.

One of the most common negative attitudes I hear is that fundraising is necessary evil. It's a miracle that anyone with this kind of attitude has ever successfully raised enough support to get them to the field! Yes, funds are necessary, if you plan to have shelter and food, if you plan to travel, if you plan to have any ministry projects, if you plan to build anything, if you plan to help those in need.

It would be wonderful if God just miraculously filled your bank account from the moment you said, "Here am I send me!" However, in my experience that's not the way God usually operates. Instant funds from the bank of God wouldn't require much trust on your part; it wouldn't require you to invite others to join you in your vision to spread the gospel; it wouldn't put you in contact with hundreds or even thousands who may not give financially but will be supporting you in prayer!

Funds are necessary! Even Jesus didn't use miracles all the time to provide for His ministry but rather they had a "money bag" (John 13:29).

His followers probably made donations to this money bag. Yes, it's likely that even God Almighty raised support for His mission. If He did it, why should you be exempt? So money is necessary, but neither the fundraising process nor the money itself are evil!

2. I don't want to beg for money.

Some assume that if you're going to raise funds then you must resort to groveling, begging type behavior. This could not be further from the truth. The Apostle Paul himself gave clear instructions to the church in Corinth about making a collection for those in Jerusalem (1 Corinthians 16:1-3). He simply made the need known and ask them to join in helping those in need.

Paul also told the Corinthians about how the brethren in Macedonia had shared generously with the saints in Jerusalem and called it type of sharing a "privilege of participating in the ministry" (2 Corinthians 8:4). You're raising funds that enable you to preach the Good News of Jesus Christ and that will allow others to hear that Good News. With that perspective, shouldn't look or feel like begging.

Begging usually implies that the person who is asking for money is not doing anything in return; he's not usefully employed in anything other than asking others for free handouts. A beggar offers no investment, not return on the the money given to him. Furthermore a beggar usually finds his most generous donors are those who don't have any kind of meaningful relationship with him. Those who know the beggar personally are probably the least likely to give to him because they may know his destructive habits.

On the other hand the missionary is not looking for free handouts. He's looking for people who would like the privilege of participating with him in Gospel ministry. The missionary is opening up his life to others; he's offering an investment that will have eternal results. The missionary is employed in the work of the Kingdom of God! Usually the missionary will find that some of his best supporters are those who know him well and are well informed about his ministry.

Fundraising for the missionary is the opposite of begging; it is opportunity to invest in eternity!

3. I'm wasting my time.

Do you really think that talking to others about the vision God has given you for sharing Jesus in a Gospel-deprived part of the world is somehow wasted time? I understand that you want to get to the field as soon as possible. You feel the need, God is tugging your heart towards the mission field, and that is good! Yet, you must not underestimate the value of the time spent before you go to the field. Earlier I talked about importance of preparation, ministry experience, and education. Time spent raising funds can also provide great value for your future ministry. Let me share with you a few ways I have seen value in fundraising.

1. It teaches you to trust God.
2. It exposes you to a wide range of churches.
3. It encourages and inspires others towards missions.
4. It gives you needed time to grow in your faith.
5. It strengthens your zeal for your particular field.
6. It puts you in contact with people who could pray for you.
7. It develops your speaking abilities.
8. It increases your patience.
9. It exercises your discipline.
10. It helps you to be bold.

These are just a few ways that God can use the time you spend fundraising to better prepare you for the mission field. If you approach this time as a vital period in your missionary career I'm sure you will find that God will make it a useful time for you.

4. Do I really need that much support?

Some missionaries struggle with justifying the amount they are required to raise by their mission agency. If you are going to a country where most people's income is significantly lower than your mission salary, it can make it harder to accept. Often missionaries say things like "We could survive on much less." While this may be true, it doesn't change the mission requirements for your support.

There are a few factors that I think are important to consider in order to have a correct outlook on this issue.

- **The financial numbers aren't a problem for God.** If God has called you and is truly leading you to a far off land as a missionary then there will be no obstacles too big for Him. The number set by your mission is nothing compared to God's riches. He can and will provide if that is His will. You must trust Him.
- **There is wisdom in numbers.** I'm sure you mission agency didn't just come up with this financial policies by chance. Through experienced they've learned what works and what doesn't. You might think that you could survive on less, and you probably could, but you're not going the mission field just to survive. You're going to the field in order serve and to preach the Gospel. Having a bit more than you need to "survive" ensures that you will have the freedom to do the work God has called you to do.
- **It's more than a salary.** It can be a little shocking for a new missionary to look at those financial requirements. However, it's important to realize that the overall amount that you must raise includes much more than just your salary. I will also likely include federal taxes, social security, health insurance, retirement fund, as well as fund for ministry.

Some helpful advice

If you've been struggling for some time to raise the support you need let's look at a few steps you can take to help ensure that you are on the right path.

1. Seek the advice your pastor and other experienced missionaries

I recommend that you talk with your pastor first. Share with him your concerns and frustrations and ask for his honest opinion. Hopefully your pastor is well informed of your missionary aspirations and has been part of the process from an early stage. As someone that knows you well and as someone who understands other pastors he might be able to pinpoint certain problems that you have not noticed. He may also be able to point you towards possible donors. If possible it might be worth it to have your pastor come along to one of your presentations and give you his evaluation.

Talking with an experienced missionary can also be valuable, especially if it's someone that has successfully raised and maintained their support levels. Pick their brain, ask them what works, find out what their approach is and learn from their wisdom.

2. Review your methods

What is your main method of support raising? Are you mainly visiting churches and looking for support from churches? Are you doing more home meetings and seeking support more from individuals? Do you have a strategy? Do you have a presentations that is clear and compelling? Are you sharing the passion God has given you in an understandable and logical way?

You can ask these questions of yourself or better yet, ask these questions of those who have heard your presentation. I find that every missionary is unique, we all have our own God-given personalities with its strengths and weaknesses. Some do better speaking to large groups, some do better speaking to a handful of people, and still others do better one on one. There are many different approaches and there is no one right approach when it comes to fundraising. You need to find the method that works will for your personality and your gifts, find the method that allows you to connect with people, share your passion, and invite them to join.

3. Consider non-traditional means of support

It could be that God is calling you to the mission field but he wants you to use "non-traditional" means of support. Throughout church history many missionaries have supported themselves through a small business, teaching, and many other work opportunities. It's likely that if you are going to a country that is not officially open to missionary activity you'll be required to have some form of employment in order to get into the country.

Think about the jobs you've had in the past and the skills God has already given you, are there any that you could use for a means of support on the mission field?

In addition to helping provide some support sometimes it's necessary to have some sort of non-religious employment to get into certain countries. Below are a few common professions that I have seen used well on the mission field either as a means of support or as a way to stay in the country.

- Teaching English as a second language (ESL)
- Teaching business, computers, or English in a college or university
- Working as tour a guide or operating a tour company
- Business consultant for small businesses
- Medical professions such as doctors and nurses
- Operating small business that employ locals

This list can go on but I think you get the idea. There are hundreds of professions and possibilities that could be used on the mission field either as way to self support or as a means to enter and live in the country.

Now what?

Now that you're at the end of the book I'm going to assume that you've read the book, you understand the Biblical issues at stake, you've talked to God about it, and you've sought wise counsel. Now it's time to make a decision and move forward. The decision you are about to make is significant. It will impact nearly every aspect of your life and the lives of those close to you. Some in your life may be resistant to your decision; they may tell you that it's not worth it, that it's dangerous, that it would be foolish to go. Once you make the decision there will surely be new difficulties that will appear in your life; there will be trials that you didn't expect; there could be significant spiritual opposition.

I'm telling you all of these things not to scare you away from making the decision to become a missionary but rather to prepare you. The fact that God is leading you down the path of missions doesn't mean that He has removed all the obstacles. There will be rivers to cross and fallen trees to climb over, there will be times when the path will be so covered with growth that the next right step will be difficult to determine. However, none of this means you're not called, it just means that the called often experience greater opposition on their journey than do those who choose to stay home.

Do you best to make your calling sure now and when you face the future times of uncertainty, discouragement, or doubt you can push forward with deeper confidence knowing that you asked the right questions, that you listened to wise counsel, and that God confirmed his calling in your life through many small and some larger evidences. Allow yourself to take strength from those who saw God's calling in your life and encouraged you along your way. Point your heart to the promises in God's Word for those who faithfully serve Jesus, verses like:

Therefore, my beloved brothers, be steadfast, immovable, always abounding in the work of the Lord, knowing that in the Lord your labor is not in vain. (1 Corinthians 15:58)

So we do not lose heart. Though our outer self is wasting away, our inner self is being renewed day by day. (2 Corinthians 4:16)

Therefore let those who suffer according to God's will entrust their souls to a faithful Creator while doing good. (1 Peter 4:19)

Yes, the missionary calling may not be an easy calling but it is worth it and it's not all hardships and trials. Missions is about about giving hope and when you give hope you receive joy in return. Missions is about building relationships that will last beyond this lifetime and enjoying some of the sweetest fellowship possible here on earth. Along with missions comes a deep peace knowing that you are a small part of God's big plan. The delight of seeing the sparkle of new life in the eyes of a new believer can't be purchased. The wonder of experiencing God's miraculous power in hearts is always worth the effort!

I've given a lot of advice in the book about missions but if there's one piece of advice that I could leave you with, if there's one piece of advice that I would tell you never to forget, if there's one piece of advice that I would say keep close to your heart in all your endeavours it would be this:

Never lose sight of Jesus!

In the busyness that can overwhelm you let the thought of Jesus be forefront. Let Him be the reason you wake in the morning and the comfort that allows you to sleep at night. Never lose sight of the fact that the mission is about Him, because of Him, and for Him. Do not make your mission primarily about a new culture, a new people, or a new language. All of those things have their place and their place is at the feet of Jesus. Don't allow yourself to be distracted by worries over finances, paperwork, health, or safety. Meditate on Jesus' goodness to you every day, grow in personal thankfulness and allow that gratitude to spill over into the lives of others. Don't neglect your own spirit, fill it before you go out to give others what you already have. Make Jesus greater, bigger, and finer than anything else in your life. Make your mission about Jesus and you will not be disappointed, make it about anything else and you are bound to experience disappointment and discouragement.

Learn to dig deeper into God's Word than ever before and allow God's Word to dig deep into you. Allow that Word to change you daily bringing you closer to Jesus. Look at every ministry, every relationship, every difficulty as an opportunity for you to trust Jesus more, to become like Him, and to bring Him glory.

Welcome!

If you are now confident that God is calling you into mission then I want to be the first to say, "Welcome!" You're not entering a high-class club or a prestigious guild of professionals. You haven't "moved up in the world," on the contrary you've moved down! You've moved down to your knees in humble service of our glorious God! You've joined a surprisingly unextraordinary fellowship of people to whom has been given an extraordinary task!

Welcome the greatest task ever given! You will have the privilege of bringing hope to the hopeless, life to the lifeless, and peace to the peaceless. You will have the joy of seeing hearts revived in faith, eyes opened to truth, and minds changed by the power of Jesus! Remain faithful to the task and the reward will be greater than you can imagine!

Your story

I wrote this book with the prayer that it will help some confirm God's calling in their lives. If you believe God is calling you into missions I would love to hear your story! You can read others' stories about how God has called them to missions and submit your own story as well at **http://sukofamily.org/IsGodCallingMe**

About the Author

Since 2007 Caleb has served as a missionary in Odessa, Ukraine where he is pastor at Hope for People Church and director of "Evangelism Today" center for evangelism and discipleship. http://blagovestie.today. Caleb attended Shasta Bible College and graduated from North West Baptist seminary in 2005 with a Master's of Divinity.

Together with his wife Christina their desire is to help believers and churches to do biblical evangelism and discipleship. This is accomplished by conducting training seminars on evangelism and discipleship for churches. It also involves personal discipleship and working closely with national pastors to help strengthen and multiply the Church in Ukraine and beyond.

The Sukos have five children.

If you'd like to learn more about the Suko's ministry please visit
http://sukofamily.org

What If...

How to Kill Worry and Anxiety Before they Kill You!

ABOUT THE BOOK

Did you know that excessive worry and anxiety can lead to real physical problems like memory loss, a weak immune system and even heart attack? Worry isn't something you can afford to ignore, it's dangerous and if you don't take care of it really could kill you!

This book will open your eyes to the shocking truth of what worry really is and where it comes from. It will expand your understanding of how worry destroys lives from the inside out. It will teach you to recognize worry it all it's ugly forms and then it will give you the tools you need to kill it before it does any more damage to your life!

Do you worry about your loved ones? If so then this book is for you. Caleb gives practical advice about how to overcome anxiety that we often experience over our children, spouses or other loved ones.

Do you worry about your possessions? In the book you'll find real examples of others who've struggled with this same issue and solid advice about how to find your way out.

Do you worry about your image? Many people struggle with anxiety over how they look and what others think of them. "What if..." Shows you where the problem really is and how to change your thinking.

Do you worry about your finances? You're certainly not alone! Consumer debt is a source of anxiety for millions of households today. But having your debts paid off doesn't mean you're exempt from worry. Caleb explains how we need to change our attitude and our actions toward money to kill worry over finances.

Do you worry about your health and safety? You'll find out that no matter how many safety precautions you take life is still a risk and often playing it safe will not ease your worries.

In his book Caleb also teaches you how to stop fretting over decisions by simplifying the processes and using the knowledge you have to make that decision and move forward with your life.

"What if..." also give you the four basic tools you need to do battle with worry every day and to become victorious.

http://sukofamily.org/whatifbook